THE QUESTION
OF CHRISTIAN ETHICS

The 1990 Michael J. McGivney Lectures
of the John Paul II Institute for Studies
on Marriage and Family

THE QUESTION
OF CHRISTIAN ETHICS

Ralph McInerny

The Catholic University of America Press
Washington, D.C.

The paper used in this publication meets the minimum requirements of American
National Standards for Information Science—Permanence of Paper for Printed
Library Materials, ANSI Z39.48–1984.
∞

LIBRARY OF CONGRESS CATALOGING-IN-PUBLICATION DATA
McInerny, Ralph M.
  The question of Christian ethics / Ralph McInerny.
    p.   cm.—(The Michael J. McGivney lectures of the John Paul
II Institute for Studies on Marriage and Family ; 1990)
  Includes bibliographical references and index.
    1. Christian ethics—Catholic authors.   I. Title.   II. Series
BJ1249.M28   1993
241'.01—dc20
92–25511
ISBN 0–8132–0770–3 (cloth). — ISBN 0–8132–0771–1 (pbk.)

For Benedict M. Ashley, O.P.

Contents

Preface

These lectures are published as they were given and thus retain the tone of talks delivered to a general audience. If non-experts can find them intelligible, it goes without saying that my fellow philosophers will find them dissatisfying. So do I. In them I address issues of the greatest importance and all I can hope to do here is to make some small contribution to their discussion. We stand, I believe, on the threshold of a great forward movement in the history of Thomism, and it is well that we debate matters essential to a proper understanding of the thought of St. Thomas. In these lectures I am chiefly concerned to prevent philosophy, more narrowly, moral philosophy, from being swallowed up by theology, but at the same time I wish to insist that it is within the ambience of the faith that philosophizing is best carried on. If I have managed to show the compatibility of these two claims, I shall be content.

I am grateful to Carl Anderson, president of the John Paul II Institute, for inviting me to give these lectures. Aware that my predecessors were John Finnis and Elizabeth Anscombe, I was at once flattered to be asked and fearful of the comparison with these superb philosophers to whom we owe so much. I want to thank the Dominican Fathers for their hospitality during my visits to Washington to deliver these lectures. Years ago, when I was admitted to the Third Order of Saint Dominic, my sponsor was Charles De Koninck, from whom I learned such Thomism as I know.

In the Ambrosiana library in Milan there is an autograph of St. Thomas Aquinas, a manuscript written in his own distinctive hand, the famous or infamous *litera inintelligibilis:* the unreadable writing. It is a portion of the third book of the *Summa Contra Gentiles.* I once had the moving experience of holding that manuscript in my hands, looking at the script which was to me *inintelligibilis* indeed. Nonetheless, I had the sense of being physically linked to the saintly Dominican who is called the Doctor Communis of the Church. Moving as that was, it is more moving still to come into contact with a living continuator of the work of St. Thomas. Thirty-eight years ago when I joined the faculty at Notre Dame, it was the custom for philosophers in the area to gather twice a year in Chicago, coming from Milwaukee, South Bend, and from the Dominican House of Studies at River Forest. From River Forest came Father Kane, Father Weisheipl, and the man to whom I dedicate these lectures. Father Benedict Ashley has in recent years been the principal pillar on which the John Paul II Institute has reposed. This is but the latest in a lifetime of contributions to the intellectual and spiritual life of the Church. (Penultimate among them, perhaps, is Father Ashley's *The Dominicans,* which appeared 1990.) I have known Father Ashley for a long time, now into a fourth decade, and my admiration for him has survived the temptation to take for granted a Dominican who lives out the vocation to which he has been called. Familiarity can breed familiarity, dulling our sense of the giants we have the privilege to know. Benedict Ashley is a giant. It is a small thing to dedicate these lectures to him—I know he would have preferred it to be a murder mystery—but I do so with affection and respect and gratitude.

RALPH MCINERNY

THE QUESTION
OF CHRISTIAN ETHICS

CHAPTER I

Is a Philosophical Ethics Possible?

Immanuel Kant stands in the forefront of those who wished to interpret Christianity as essentially a moral teaching separable from the mythical, cosmological, and dogmatic baggage that encumbers it.[1] The Christian message, thus saved, turns out to have no essential relationship to Christ—he just happened to recommend it, but, correctly understood, that doctrine is what any rational agent would come to see as his duty.

In sharp contrast to this is the position that the moral message of Christianity is so essentially linked with the complete package of Revelation that all attempts to separate it from that wider context are futile. Moreover, since Christianity alone addresses human beings as they actually are, revealing to them their true destiny and good, there is no way, apart from Christianity, that we can know our true good. Thus, the suggestion that Christianity can be reduced to a moral message accessible to all independently of its historical clothing—and indeed of any essential relation to Jesus—is fundamentally wrongheaded, since there is no true knowledge of the human good apart from Revelation.[2]

Is there or is there not a philosophical ethics alongside of and irreducible to the Way, the Truth, and the Life that is Jesus Christ? And first, what kind of a question is this? We can't imagine Mother Teresa tossing and turning through sleepless nights,

1. Immanuel Kant, *Religion within the Limits of Reason Alone*, trans., with intro. and notes, by John R. Silber (New York, Harper; 1960).

2. See John Calvin, *Institutes of the Christian Religion*, trans. Ford Lewis Battles (Grand Rapids: Eerdmans, 1986). On this question generally, see *Is There A Christian Ethics?* by Lucien Richard, O.M.I. (New York: Paulist Press, 1988).

wondering how to answer it. I have relatives who haven't devoted half a minute to it. Let them stand for the majority of
Christian believers. The question is not obligatory, high on everyone's agenda, as if a day could not begin until it is settled. For
that matter, neither Plato nor Aristotle formulated it. How could
they have? The question requires a contrast that is given only
when one imagines two distinct, perhaps rival, moral doctrines
and asks if they are both true, or one true and the other false. In
the history of Christianity the question arises sharply when, over
and against Revelation and the tradition of reflecting upon and
interpretating Revelation, another doctrine, one with its origins
in pagan thought, makes its appearance.

Toward the end of the twelfth century, a century noteworthy
for its efforts to codify and collect the Christian intellectual tradition, efforts that issued in the Code of Gratian, the *Glossa Ordi-
naria* and the *Sentences* of Peter Lombard, disturbing intellectual
novelties began to infiltrate from Toledo and elsewhere. Books
Two and Three of Aristotle's *Nicomachean Ethics* found their
way into Latin, and then Book One was added to them, but it
was Robert Grosseteste who provided the first complete Latin
version of Aristotle's masterful ethical work, and it soon became
a basis for teaching in the Faculty of Arts at the University of
Paris.

The Faculty of Arts began as a continuation of the liberal arts
curriculum that had characterized medieval education. In the
sixth century, when Cassiodorus Senator wrote his *Institutiones*
for the monks of Vivarium, the monastery he founded, he distinguished between sacred and secular learning.[3] Secular learning
was conveniently summed up in the liberal arts, which were
divided into the arts of the trivium and the arts of the quadri-
vium. A threefold way and a fourfold way, but ways to what? To
wisdom, to the truth revealed by God in Holy Scripture. Some of
the *auctores* of the arts were pagans, but the skills they taught, in
grammar and logic and rhetoric, in arithmetic, geometry, music,

3. Cassiodorus Senator, *Institutiones divinarum et humanarum lectionum*, ed.
R. A. Mynors (Oxford: Clarendon Press, 1937).

and astronomy, were considered to be all but necessary for the appropriate understanding of the Bible.

The liberal arts tradition thus embodies a view of the relationship between secular and sacred learning. The view would seem clearly to be that there are arts or skills that any human person, believer or nonbeliever, can acquire. The believer sees them as instrumentally useful for a further purpose, but that does not alter the autonomous nature of the liberal arts.

Of course there have always been believers who regarded this use of secular learning in interpretating Revelation as dangerous. Bernard of Clairvaux's opposition to Peter Abelard was a particularly dramatic instance of a continuing argument between dialecticians and nondialecticians.[4]

The liberal arts only inadequately represent what the Greeks meant by philosophy.[5] The disputes between dialecticians and nondialecticians until the end of the twelfth century went on in almost total ignorance of the scope and dimensions of pagan philosophy. From the time of Boethius until the latter part of the twelfth century, for over seven hundred years, Aristotle was known only in a few of his logical works, and Plato only in a translation of the *Timaeus*. That a good deal of indirect knowledge of Greek philosophy was had via the Fathers does not alter the fact that direct contact with pagan philosophy was minimal.

And then something most dramatic happened. From various translation centers, fostered by a variety of patrons (not at all an organized effort), streams arose and eventually converged until what must have seemed a flood of translations roared into Christian centers of learning, Paris and Naples and Oxford.[6] These translations of Aristotle, as well as of such Islamic masters as

4. See Ralph McInerny, *A History of Western Philosophy* 2 (Notre Dame: University of Notre Dame Press, 1970), pp. 119–21, 140–56, 195–97.
5. See my essay, "Beyond the Liberal Arts," in David L. Wagner, ed., *The Seven Liberal Arts in the Middle Ages* (Bloomington: Indiana University Press, 1986), pp. 248–72.
6. Fernand van Steenberghen, *Aristotle in the West,* trans. Leonard Johnston, 2d ed. (Louvain: Nauwelaerts, 1970).

Avicenna and Averroes, created a radically different cultural and intellectual situation in the thirteenth century.

The long tradition of Christian learning stemming from the Fathers (most notably Augustine) and taking its shape in the monastic schools and eventually the cathedral schools, represented an enormous achievement. This Augustinian tradition incorporated within it a view of the relation between what God has revealed and what pagan philosophers had taught. That relation can be summed up in the phrase *praeparatio evangelica*—pagan learning seen as a prelude to the Gospel, in some ways an adumbration of it.[7] Indeed, Augustine himself long entertained the thought that Plato had been influenced by Judaism, so impressed was he by Plato's putative affinity to the faith. In a famous passage, Augustine interpreted the Platonic forms in such a way that one could not be a Christian and reject them. Taking the forms to be the creative patterns in the mind of God, Augustine suggested that to reject the ideas was tantamount to saying that God did not know what he was doing when he created.[8] In retrospect, Augustine thought he had been overly enthusiastic in his embrace of Platonism, but he did not take back the suggestion that philosophy at its best, far from being inimical to the faith, could be seen as its complement, however inadequate and groping it must appear to the eye of the believer.[9] In another famous remark, he suggested that the Christian could take the treasures of philosophy from the pagans as from unjust or unworthy possessors. It is a truth, though not the whole truth, of the Augustinian tradition, which dominated Christian thought well into the thirteenth Century, that it regarded philosophy not as a rival or an enemy but as an ally of sorts.

With the influx of a vast library of hitherto unread Aristotelian works, the question of the relation of faith and reason had to be

7. See Etienne Gilson, *History of Christian Philosophy in the Middle Ages* (New York: Random House, 1955), pp. 9–64.
8. St. Augustine, *83 Diverse Questions,* q. 46; cf. St. Thomas, *Summa theologiae,* Ia, q. 15.
9. *Retractationes,* III,2.

reopened and the thirteenth century is the time when the great battles were fought. Was pagan philosophy, now almost identical with Aristotle, to be regarded as the foe of, the false alternative to, Christianity, or could some such solution as that embodied in Cassiodorus be worked out, not this time between the liberal arts and Revelation, but between Aristotelian philosophy in all its amplitude, on the one hand, and Revelation, along with the traditional, Augustinian way of reflecting on it, on the other?[10]

In the twelfth century, Abelard could write a *Dialogue Between a Philosopher, a Jew and a Christian,* suggesting that the truths of the philosopher, like those of the Jew, are to be found in their fullness in Christianity, but the question could scarcely pose itself for Abelard's *dramatis personae* as it did for, say, Dominic Gundassalinus. In Toledo, under the auspices of the archbishop, Christian, Jew, and Moslem brought together in living form the three religions of the Book as they jointly translated into Latin the pagan philosophy of Aristotle. Jewish and Moslem efforts to relate that philosophy to religious belief thus became known. Avicenna in Bagdad, Maimonides in Cairo, Averroes in Cordoba, had already confronted their versions of the question that came to a head in the thirteenth century at the University of Paris.[11]

It was easy to see logic and mathematics as independent of religious truth, but things were considerably different when the Christian was confronted with pagans speaking of the human soul and its survival of death, or of the relationship between the cosmos and God. Some wished to adopt what could be called the apples and oranges approach: There is no comparison between what philosophers say and believers believe. Philosophical truth is one thing, theological truth another, and there is no need to choose between the two.[12]

10. See the article cited in n. 5, above.
11. See the dedicatory letter to the bishop of Toledo by Avendeuth, a Jewish philosopher, in *Avicenna Latinus,* crit. ed. S. van Riet, vol. 1 (Louvain: E. Peeters, 1972), pp. 3–6.
12. This is the position attributed to Siger of Brabant, not wholly unjustly. Cf.

That approach would have been more attractive if it did not seem that what philosophers were saying contradicts what believers believe. Thus, on the basis of Genesis, believers hold that the world and time had a beginning, but Aristotle maintained that the world had always existed and could not come to be. Moreover, Aristotle was taken to say that God is ignorant of the world, whereas believers know that his eye is on the sparrow. Clearly, if what the believer believes is true, what Aristotle teaches is false. Thomas Aquinas was at the center of this discussion and came up with a resolution of such issues that, whatever its immediate historical fate, came to be the outlook adopted by the Catholic Church.[13]

Thomas's approach can be generally characterized as assuming that, when Aristotle is correctly understood, his teachings can be seen to be compatible with the faith. He played a crucial role in the discussion of the "errors of Aristotle," around which controversy swirled in the thirteenth century. Aristotle was, in Thomas's eyes, both a mentor and an ally on key questions in metaphysics and psychology and theory of knowledge. What about moral philosophy?

The Reformers, whose estimate of Aristotle was not flattering and who gave correspondingly low marks to the Scholasticism that had assimilated Aristotle, may be expected to frown on the suggestion that sinful man can, by his own flawed powers and without the grace of God, discover the moral good. The Protestant rejection of the natural moral law is but one obvious consequence of this attitude. The Catholic thinker can be expected to maintain the human mind's ability, even in a condition of sin, to grasp truths of the moral as well as speculative order. So linked has the Church become with the defense of natural law that the

Bernardo Carlos Bazán's *Siger de Brabant. Quaestiones in tertium de anima. De anima intellectiva. De aeternitate mundi* (Louvain: Nauwelaerts, 1972).

13. See, for example, Thomas Aquinas, *On There Being Only One Intellect,* trans., with intro. and comm., Ralph McInerny (Lafayette, Indiana: Purdue University Press, 1992).

doctrine is often and wrongly described as a Catholic one. Wrongly, if by that is meant that the acceptance of natural law depends intriniscally on the acceptance of revealed truth. Were that the case, the whole point of natural law would thereby be lost. Natural law is the claim that all human agents, believers and nonbelievers alike, can grasp basic truths of the moral order, that not even the most heinous personal or social sin can completely eradicate such a possibility from the human mind.[14] Among Catholics, Thomists are particular champions of the moral natural law, always ready to explain, defend, and expand the Angelic Doctor's teaching on this point.

It must come as a surprise, therefore, to find that some of the most eminent Thomists of our day have called into question the very possibility of a philosophical ethics. Jacques Maritain, as we shall see, was among them and, in the words of Vernon Bourke, "My old professor, Etienne Gilson, came to agree with Maritain that a purely philosophical ethics is of little practical value."[15]

The Medieval Model

Maritain and Gilson were, of course, two of the foremost figures in the Thomistic Revival which grew out of Leo XIII's 1879 encyclical *Aeterni Patris*. The Holy Father had urged Catholics to return to the great tradition represented by, but not identical with, the teaching of Thomas Aquinas. The story of the personal and institutional responses to this and later papal encyclicals dealing with Thomism is rich and complicated and has only begun to be written. There are local and regional histories, many of which began to be explored in 1974 during the multiple and global commemorations of the 700th anniversary of the death of Thomas Aquinas.[16] The comprehensive account is yet to

14. See *Summa theologiae,* IaIIae, q. 94, a. 6.
15. *Thomist* 40, (1976), p. 555.
16. For example, *Veritas et Sapientia: En el vii Centenario de Santo Tomás de Aquino* (Pamplona: University of Navarre, 1975); Congresso Internazionale:

be written, but when it is it will surely be one of the most glorious chapters in the history of Thomism. And prominent in that account will be the names of Jacques Maritain and Etienne Gilson.

The history of the study of medieval philosophy since 1879 is in itself fascinating. Today, when programs in medieval studies are commonplace, when few universities would care to be without courses in medieval philosophy, it is difficult to imagine a period when those centuries languished in obscurity or were objects of obloquy—if they were remembered at all. The Enlightenment had led mankind through the waters of Lethe, the priest-ridden days of yore were blotted from the mind, the reign of Reason had begun. By the time of Leo XIII, long before the Guns of August, it was clear where the Enlightenment was taking mankind. Clear at least to Leo XIII. When he wrote his encyclical, it was imaginable that the sons and daughters of the Enlightenment thought that they had triumphed. The pope, by contrast, lived as if under siege, speaking for and to a people scattered over the earth, seeming captives of outmoded and superstitious beliefs. Christians lived, as it were, in diaspora, surrounded by a liberalism inimical to their faith, themselves inevitably influenced in thought and action by that ambience, understandably trying to work out compromises with the Zeitgeist. The century and more since the appearance of Leo's encyclical have vindicated his assessment of the intellectual and cultural milieu of his time. The drama of modern thought has culminated in the rejection of the Reason it began by celebrating. Intellectual nihilism is fashionable.[17] Thanks to the revival Leo XIII fostered, the intellectual means of our deliverance are at hand.

Tommaso D'Aquino nel suo VII Centenario (Rome and Naples, 1974); *Atti del Congresso Internazionale,* 9 vols. (Naples: Edizioni Domenicane Italiane, 1975–78).

17. Friedrich Nietzsche (1844–1900) was living in St. Moritz when *Aeterni Patris* appeared. It is doubtful that he knew of it or that Leo XIII knew of him. At the time Nietzsche was regarded as a marginal figure rather than as representative of the essence of modernity. In 1945, Jean-Paul Sartre's *Existentialism Is a Humanism* drew the lines clearly. Today we have the urbane and insidious Richard Rorty. See *Contingency, Irony and Solidarity* (New York: Cambridge University Press, 1990).

One of the first and most influential histories of medieval philosophy to appear in the Thomistic Revival tried to see the Christian thinkers of the Middle Ages as maintaining a single unitary view, one that can be dubbed Scholasticism. Despite particular emphases or deviations, the thought of the Middle Ages was somehow one: there was fundamental agreement among Christian medieval thinkers. This was a view Etienne Gilson contested with energy and wit, writing a series of books on the chief figures involved—Thomas Aquinas, Bonaventure, Scotus—as well as on Augustine. The result, if not his purpose, was to display the deep differences that divided the thirteenth-century figures from one another: they did not possess a common philosophy; there are many medieval philosophies, not one, as Maurice De Wulf had maintained.[18]

Gilson spoke as an historian who was not willing to pass beyond the palpable differences between a Thomas and a Bonaventure to some putative common view beyond. Taken in their historical concreteness, it is impossible to confuse Thomas with Bonaventure and vice versa. Once their difference could be easily seen by comparing the prayers of the two saints contained at the beginning of the *Missale Romanum*. A comparison of *Itinerarium mentis ad Deum* and the *De ente et essentia,* while more demanding, makes the differences between the two minds palpable. And even when the commentaries each man wrote on the *Sentences* of Peter Lombard, an exercise by definition impersonal and scholastic, are compared, the profound differences between them are unavoidable.

Something that must not be overlooked, Gilson insisted, is that the men to whom we refer were all theologians.[19] In the case of Bonaventure, it would be difficult to find among his works any that could be called philosophical, or purely philosophical. The same cannot be said of Thomas, but no matter. He too was a

18. In his famous *Histoire de la philosophie médiévale,* 6th ed. (Louvain: Nauwelaerts, 1936).
19. See *History of Christian Philosophy in the Middle Ages* (New York: Random House, 1955).

theologian, not a philosopher. Now you might think that, from all this, Gilson would have concluded that what was going on in the medieval period was theology, not philosophy. If he had concluded this, he would have been in agreement with Bertrand Russell and Will Durant and other eminent historians of philosophy who held that nothing philosophical had happened during that thousand years we call the Middle Ages. Gilson actually concluded something else.

Philosophy during the Middle Ages, he said, was not an activity carried on independently of theology. The philosophy of a thinker like Bonaventure is embedded in his theology, and the same is true of the philosophy of Thomas Aquinas. Such men, in short, developed a Christian philosophy, not to be confused with their theology, even though it was done in the course of their theologizing. Theology and philosophy might be distinct, but they are not separate. So much is this the case that the proper order of the philosophy of Thomas is the same as the proper order of his theology. That is, the order of Thomistic philosophy is precisely the order of the *Summa theologiae*.[20] Thus was defined the controversy over Christian philosophy, a controversy that provides the setting for the problem I address in these lectures: Is there or is there not a philosophical ethics distinct from moral theology?

The controversy over Christian philosophy seemed to complicate the question. No longer was a distinction made simply between theology and philosophy. Now, between the two, a *tertium quid* was posited, neither theology nor philosophy as the pagan engaged in it, a philosophy that found its home in the Christian era and was unintelligible apart from that setting, namely, Christian philosophy. The question of this lecture is no longer simply whether there is an ethics or moral philosophy independent of moral theology. Now the question becomes: Is it only as an instance of Christian philosophy that an ethics distinct

---

20. This was questioned by James Collins in "Toward a Philosophically Ordered Thomism," *New Scholasticism* 32 (1958), pp. 301–26.

from moral theology can be recognized? But what is Christian philosophy?

Christian Philosophy

The concept of Christian philosophy was put forward by Gilson at the very outset of his Gifford Lectures, *The Spirit of Mediaeval Philosophy*.[21] Indeed, the first two chapters discuss the notion of Christian philosophy as a prelude to the central theme of Gilson's lectures. In order to put before his listeners the spirit of medieval philosophy, Gilson had to indicate how the ambience within which thinking went on in those centuries differed from that of modern times. By way of contrast, he spoke of the rationalist, one who regards philosophy as something to be carried on without reference to anything other than itself. "Surely philosophical arguments are independent of extraneous considerations," the rationalist may be imagined to say. But Gilson is not concerned only with what he calls the pure rationalist. There is another figure on the scene, one Gilson calls the neo-scholastic, a Christian, indeed a Thomist, who, in Gilson's eyes, adopts the position of his opponents and effectively says that the only genuine philosophy in the Middle Ages was that of Thomas Aquinas. Thomas is the only one who qualifies as a pure philosopher. Anselm and Bonaventure "take their stand on faith, and therefore they shut themselves up in theology" (5).

In Thomism alone we have a system in which philosophic conclusions are deduced from purely rational premises. Theology remains in its proper place, that is to say at the head of a hierarchy of the sciences; based on divine revelation, from which it receives its principles, it constitutes a distinct science starting from faith and turning to reason only to draw out the content of faith and to protect it from error. Philosophy, doubtless, is subordinate to theology, but, as philosophy, it depends on nothing but its own proper method; based on human reason, owing all

---

21. Etienne Gilson, *The Spirit of Mediaeval Philosophy* (Gifford Lectures 1931–1932), trans. A. H. C. Downes (New York: Charles Scribner's Sons, 1936); hereafter cited in the text.

its truth to the self-evidence of its principles and the accuracy of its deductions, it reaches an accord with faith spontaneously and without having to deviate in any way from its own proper path. (6)

Such a Thomist takes any conflict between his faith and his philosophy as a certain sign of philosophical error. "If, however, even then he fails to come to an understanding with the rationalist, it is not for lack of speaking the same language" (6). The truth of his philosophy depends on faith no more than the rationalist's.

It is against this personage that Gilson directs the criticism of those medieval Augustinians who saw in Thomism "the paganization of Christianity." The modern Thomist who denies that Augustinianism is a genuine philosophy, because of its appeal to faith, is reminded that he will be accused of infidelity to the Christian tradition. The accusation is tantamount to saying that Thomism so understood is not a Christian philosophy. Gilson's purpose in discussing Christian philosophy is to suggest not only that Thomism, correctly understood, is a Christian philosophy, but also that the thought of Bonaventure and other Augustinians can be recognized as equally deserving of the appellation Christian philosophy.

Christian philosophy will be intelligible in the light of one's view of the relationship of faith and reason. The Thomist of whom Gilson clearly disapproves considers faith extrinsic to reason. Is Gilson suggesting that faith can be intrinsic to philosophy? The answer is clearly yes, but he has yet to clarify whether faith is intrinsic to the essence or to the exercise of philosophy (9).

In the second chapter of *The Spirit of Mediaeval Philosophy*, Gilson embarks on a historical search for an answer to the question: What did the acceptance of faith do for the philosophy of philosophers who became Christian? He looks first at Paul and then at Justin, who found in the faith the wisdom he had sought in vain in philosophy. Nonetheless, in becoming a Christian Justin felt that he had truly become a philosopher. Paul, in the Epistle to the Romans (1.19–20), by saying that the pagan Romans could, from the things that are made, come to knowledge of the invisible things of God, laid "the foundation of all the natural theologies which will later arise in the bosom of Christianity" (26). So too the Apostle spoke of a natural moral law (2.14–15) or rather, Gilson suggests, "a natural knowledge of the moral law" (26). These texts were bound to give rise to the question: What is the relationship between our rational, God-given knowledge of the true and the good, and revealed knowledge? Justin gave an answer which Gilson phrases thus: "On the testimony of God Himself, we must admit a natural revelation of the Word, universal and antedating the revelation given when He took flesh and dwelt amongst us" (27). All who participate in the light of the Word, through whichever revelation, participate in the light of Christ; this has the surprising implication that pagans and Jews who lived according to the Word were Christians! From the perspective of the faith, Christianity can dispense with philosophy or supersede it by being its fulfillment. Thus it was that Christians scolded the philosophers for their confusions and disagreements.

The upshot of Gilson's historical survey is to validate the claim that there is a Christian philosophy, because acceptance of the faith was taken to confer philosophical advantages as well as others. Christian philosophy requires that there be an intrinsic relationship between Revelation and reason. This does not mean that "faith is a kind of cognition superior to rational cognition" (35). Nor does it mean that, proceeding from premises of faith, you can arrive at a conclusion that is pure science. Neither the theologian nor the Christian philosopher seeks to transform faith into knowledge, "as if by some queer chemistry you could combine contradictory essences" (36). Rather, the Christian asks whether, among the truths he accepts on faith, there are any he can know by reason to be true. If there are, there is a progression from faith to knowledge, and the latter can be called Christian philosophy because of the original status of the truth for the believer.

This is an extremely important point, whether or not we think that Gilson's use of the phrase Christian philosophy always conforms to it. Among the truths proposed for our belief are some that we can come to *know* are true. Thomas called such truths *praeambula fidei*.[22] On this understanding of Christian philosophy, the adjective refers to the starting point in faith of truths one comes to know, that is, to hold as true on a basis other than faith, a basis available to believer and nonbeliever alike. Gilson would not call Christian a philosophy that is simply open to the supernatural, that does not exclude it as a possibility. "If it is to deserve that name the supernatural must descend as a constitutive element not, of course, into its texture which would be a contradiction, but into the work of its construction. Thus I call Christian, *every philosophy which, although keeping the two orders formally distinct, nevertheless considers the Christian revelation as an indispensable auxiliary to reason*" (38). Gilson thus takes to be essential to the concept of Christian philosophy the provenance in the faith of certain truths. Here he finds a device for joining together a great many different philosophies because they all exhibit the influence of Christianity in their construction.

One of the marks of Christian philosophy will be the questions it chooses to treat; by and large, they will be questions that affect the conduct of the religious life. Perhaps remembering that it would be difficult so to restrict the philosophical work of Thomas, Gilson somewhat enigmatically suggests that Thomas did his "creative work only in a relatively restricted sphere"[23]— by which he means, on problems that affect the conduct of the religious life. This is not surprising, since the revelation from

22. As, for example, in his exposition of Boethius's *De trinitate* (ed. Decker), q. II, art. iii, p. 94, line 28, and *Summa theologiae*, Ia, q. 2, a. 2, ad 1m.

23. "There is no question of minimizing his merits as a commentator and interpreter of Aristotle; it is not in that field, however, that he is greatest, but rather in those genial views in which he prolonged and surpassed the philosophic effort of Aristotle. And these views are almost always to be found when he is speaking of God and of the soul and of the relations between God and soul. The deepest of them have to be disentangled from the theological contexts in which they are embedded, for it is there, in the bosom of theology, that they effectively come to birth. In a word, faith has a simplifying influence on all Christian philosophers worthy of the name, and their originality shines forth especially in the sphere directly influenced by faith, that is to say in the doctrine concerning God and man, and man's relations to God" (38).

which Christian philosophy takes its rise teaches us only truths necessary for salvation (38). Man's relation to God is the central theme of Christian philosophy.

Somewhat surprisingly, perhaps, Gilson concludes by insisting that a "true philosophy, taken absolutely and in itself, owes all its truth to its rationality and to nothing other than its rationality." Nonetheless, "the constitution of this true philosophy could not in fact be achieved without the aid of revelation, acting as an indispensable moral support to reason" (40–41). It is this that gives meaning to the phrase Christian philosophy. In the abstract, philosophy professes no religion, but it is not a matter of indifference that the philosopher does.

Gilson's presentation of the concept of Christian philosophy generated an enormous amount of discussion. The second meeting of the French Thomistic Society, held at Juvisy in September 1933, was devoted to the question.[24] Magnificent papers by Aimé Forest and Father Motte were discussed by Thomists whose names were to become, if they were not already, legendary: Chenu, Sertillanges, Van Steenberghen, Jolivet, Festugière, Mandonnet, de Solages, Feuling, Dopp, Masnovo, and Gilson himself. The exchange between Gilson and Mandonnet[25] is particularly instructive because it set forth what were to be the continuing parameters of the debate. Thomists at Juvisy were deeply divided on the question of Christian philosophy: Some would keep the name while proposing a weaker definition than Gilson's. Others thought the phrase itself was systematically misleading. If there was any agreement, it had to do with the influence of faith on the believing philosopher and his exercise or use of his reason.[26]

24. *La Philosophie Chrétienne*, Journées d'études de la Société Thomiste, Juvisy, September 11, 1933 (Juvisy: Les Editions du Cerf, 1934).

25. Ibid., pp. 62–72.

26. The published proceedings of the conference contains a bibliography of works dealing with the question of Christian philosophy during the period beginning with the March 21, 1931, meeting of the Société Française de Philosophie and continuing through the end of 1933. Emile Bréhier's "Y-a-t-il une philoso-

This schematic discussion of Christian philosophy provides the setting for my question: Is a philosophical ethics possible? Father Motte agrees with Gilson that philosophical discussions of God benefit from firm assertions of the faith. He adds that this is even more the case when it is a question of human moral action.[27] Operating with insufficient knowledge of man's end, moral philosophy has a limited and humble task; but everyone, Father Motte suggests, recognizes the benefits moral philosophy has received from Christianity. Among them would surely be numbered Jacques Maritain, but Father Motte does not find acceptable Maritain's notion of "moral philosophy adequately considered," which must be subalternated to theology. Be that as it may, it would be difficult to find a more formidable obstacle to an affirmative answer to my question.

Moral Philosophy Adequately Considered

Practical knowledge aims at the regulation of the concrete act, and this will be true of moral philosophy and moral theology even at the level of generality. Maritain distinguishes between two levels of practical science, one speculatively-practical, the other practically-practical, both of which are opposed to prudence, the here and now direction of this act. For purposes of our consideration now, there is no need to discuss Maritain's subdivision of moral science. He has phrased a version of our question

---

phie chrétienne?" delivered at the March 21, 1931, meeting and later published in *Révue de métaphysique et morale*, 38 (1931), pp. 133–62, and Gilson's *The Spirit of Mediaeval Philosophy* set the stage for the discussion.

27. "Mais le besoin de lumière supérieure ne fait que croître quand on passe de l'ordre des natures à celui des fins. Le mystère de Dieu se retrouve ici, mais alors que dans le cas précédent, sous les espèces de la puissance obédientielle, il n'intervenait pour ainsi dire qu'en dernier lieu, à la lisière de la nature, on le rencontre ici dès le départ dans la détermination de la fin ultime; de ce fait la philosophie morale se trouve plus entravée encore que les autres parties de la philosophie: une doctrine achevée de la conduite humaine ne peut être demandée qu'à la théologie, seule informée de la vocation surnaturelle de l'homme. Aussi comprend-on que la philosophie morale, ainsi limitée, bénéficie, en tous les éléments qui sont de son ressort, de l'influence chrétienne." Op. cit., n. 24, pp. 102–3.

as follows: In man's actual circumstances, can a purely philosophical morality form a true practical science? His answer to this question is No.[28]

A purely philosophical ethics would be possible in a state of pure nature, but in the fallen and redeemed nature that is actually ours, such an ethics could indeed prescribe good acts—that is, tell us not to lie, not to be unjust, etc.—but the prescription of good acts is not enough to form a practical science. A "true science of the use of freedom" not only prescribes good actions but "determines how the *acting subject* can live a life of consistent goodness and organize rightly his whole universe of action."[29] A purely philosophical ethics is incapable of *making a man live well* and that is why it cannot form a true practical science. Moreover, to the degree it was successful, it would tell us how a creature who does not exist might become good. Even if it enjoined us to love God above all things by natural love, we would be unable in our fallen state to do this. One who attempted to follow such an ethics would be led astray. Maritain contrasts the omissions or inadequacy of philosophical morals with those of natural theology. The latter is a speculative not a practical science, and the fact that it can know nothing of the Trinity renders its knowledge of God insufficient but does not falsify the divine nature. But ethics purports to be a practical science. "It is *essentially* insufficient in the sense that no science directive of human conduct—no science pure and simple worthy of the name—can exist without taking into account the real and actual last end of human life."[30] Maritain does not deny that natural ethics really exists. Indeed, he admits that it provides precious truths and notional instruments to the theologian. But such moral philosophy, inade-

28. See *Science and Wisdom*, trans. Bernard Wall (New York: Scribner's, 1940), especially Part Two. Both in the text and in the appendices, Maritain takes into account objections to his earlier statements about moral philosophy adequately considered. There is no more thorough discussion than that to be found in Ralph Carl Nelson, *Jacques Maritain's Conception of Moral Philosophy Adequately Considered*, a doctoral dissertation written under the direction of Joseph Evans and presented at the University of Notre Dame in 1961.

29. *Science and Wisdom*, p. 162.

30. Ibid., p. 165.

quately considered—inadequate as a guide for action—is more a sketch of a science than a developed one. Maritain also concedes that, insofar as a purely philosophical ethics is based on experience, this must be the experience of real men, not men as they might be in a state of pure nature, but then "something more than what is purely natural will enter into his philosophy: though in an obscure and implicit way, because he is not able to discern it."[31] If one does try to conceptualize it all in a "texture of *pure reason*" he will produce a false morality, "designed for man as he is but with its axis all awry."[32]

So there it is. There can be no philosophical ethics that could succeed in being the practical science it seeks to be. Does Maritain think there is only moral theology, a practical science, which would take as its principle the revealed supernatural end of man? Not at all. What he proposes is a "moral philosophy adequately considered," a moral philosophy adequate to the practical task, thanks to being subalternated to theology and thus to the faith.

It is important to note that Maritain does not deny that man has a natural as well as a supernatural end. There are natural and temporal ends of human life that are neither pure means to a life of grace and glory nor specified by the supernatural last end.[33] Nonetheless, "man only orders his life effectively to his natural last end if he keeps his eyes also on his supernatural last end."[34] So too, Maritain will affirm that moral philosophy has human acts in the widest sense as its subject matter, but he takes this to mean that human acts will be seen with reference to both of man's concrete ends, natural and supernatural. "But then, it goes without saying that as soon as the validity of moral philosophy as a practical science has been recognized, it is *ipso facto* subordinated to theology."[35]

31. Ibid., p. 167.
32. "Aristotle escaped this misfortune in some degree only because of the unsystematic character of his ethics: more prudent than the Epicurean and the Stoic, it appears rather as a series of sketches and partial pictures (sometimes very elaborate) than as an organically constituted science." Ibid., p. 167.
33. Ibid., p. 179.   34. Ibid., p. 182.
35. Ibid. Maritain holds that pure philosophy in the speculative order is ade-

The Thomist is confronted by the disturbing fact that two of the most important figures in the revival of the thought of Thomas Aquinas, Etienne Gilson and Jacques Maritain, hold views on moral philosophy that are surprisingly hostile to its autonomy. Gilson, invoking his understanding of Christian philosophy, seems to restrict the task of the Christian philosopher to the developing of arguments on behalf of those truths which, although they have been revealed and are first believed, can come to be understood. I suggested earlier that such truths are those Thomas calls the *praeambula fidei*. If we extend this concept to revealed truths of the practical order, as we can, Gilson's Christian philosopher would likely develop arguments in defense of the non-gainsayability of those precepts of natural law that are expressed in the Decalogue. It is unclear that this would result in what Maritain calls "moral philosophy adequately considered," since Gilson's Christian philosophy stresses the provenance of certain truths, not their status as philosophically established. Maritain, insofar as he allows that moral philosophy can be adequate as a practical science, speaks of it as being subalternated to moral theology. Subalternation is a technical term within Thomism and would seem to carry the dependence of moral philosophy on faith beyond anything that Gilson suggested. But in either case, we are confronted with a negative answer to my thematic question: Is a philosophical ethics possible? These lectures, taken as a whole, are meant to provide an affirmative answer to that question, and it seemed important to lay before you the formidable obstacles I face in developing that answer. In doing so, I shall be developing as well what I take to be true and important in what Gilson and Maritain have had to say, even while I reject many of the implications they take those truths to have. I shall be particularly concerned to provide what I take to be a defensible sense of Christian philosophy. It was

---

quate to its object despite the fact that man has been elevatated to the supernatural order. Only in the case of practical philosophy is it necessary for there to be subalternation to theology. See ibid., p. 184.

Gilson who observed, in the discussions at Juvisy, that *Aeterni Patris* has often been titled in translation *On Christian Philosophy*. It would be an odd Thomist who could not accept the title of the encyclical that was the cornerstone of the modern revival of interest in the thought of St. Thomas Aquinas.

CHAPTER II

Does Man Have a Natural Ultimate End?

We have seen that a number of eminent Thomists maintain that there can be no autonomous philosophical ethics that would be adequate to man as he exists. In the case of Etienne Gilson, a more comprehensive conception of Christian philosophy suggested a version of Thomism that would bring all philosophical thinking under the essential influence of the faith, including, of course, philosophical ethics. Jacques Maritain, on the other hand, noting the difference between the speculative and practical orders, restricted his judgment of the inadequacy of philosophical thinking to the realm of morality, where directives for action that fail to take into account man's supernatural end must mislead rather than lead.

The two sides of the issue can be conveniently simplified as follows: Man as he actually exists has been redeemed by Christ and called to a happiness that exceeds his natural reach, yet it is only through faith that one can accept this claim as true; therefore, moral directives adequate to actually existing man must presuppose the faith. On the other hand, it would be maintained that, although man has been called to a higher, supernatural end, this elevation of his nature does not destroy it, so that it remains possible to come to knowledge of the good perfective of the human agent and to formulate directives in the light of that natural end.

The dispute seemingly could be resolved in a quince by noting the fact that, prior to and/or independently of moral directives formulated in the light of man's supernatural end, pagan philosophers developed an ethical doctrine. In fact, there are several moral philosophies. That plurality seems to tell against the success of the effort. Proponents of a moral philosophy do not consider its rivals equally true. But there are ways in which disputes between rival ethics can be adjudicated and the various ethics ranked as to adequacy without appeal to the human vocation that has been divinely revealed. Nor should it be overlooked that ethical theories and systems have multiplied in the post-Christian period of Western philosophy. That these latter-day systems may not be as liberated from Christian influence, even of a positive kind, as they imagine, is a familiar observation. Nevertheless, the various ethical theories studied in philosophy survey courses purport to be, and indeed are, efforts to base moral guidance on reason alone. When one takes exception to a claim in one of them, or to a whole system of morality, the criticism need not be based on the faith.

When an ethics has been developed by a philosopher who is a pagan, someone like Plato or Aristotle, it would of course be anachronistic to ask what their view of the relation between moral philosophy and Christianity is. True, this is a question that might have been put to them by Dante, but the answer would come from an imaginary rather than an historical character. Nonetheless, we ourselves can pose the question of the relation between philosophical ethics and moral theology, and in two quite distinct ways. First, we can ask whether the philosophical ethics developed by Aristotle precludes man's elevation to a supernatural end. Is Aristotelian ethics a rival to or a substitute for moral theology? Again, it is *we* who put the question, not Aristotle. Is Maritain's portrayal of Aristotle's ethics justified? (In *Science and Wisdom* it is scarcely more than an aside.)

Second, the question can be put from the side of moral theology. Given our supernatural end, is it not the case that moral theology can treat the human agent as a whole and thus that whatever meager truths the philosophers hit upon will show up in moral theology in a far stronger and more defensible form? That is, in the present dispensation, hasn't philosophical ethics been rendered otiose?

The Ethics of Aristotle

We have the great advantage in having been preceded in the posing and pursuit of these questions by St. Thomas Aquinas. At the outset of the Second Part of the *Summa theologiae,* the moral part, in a series of five questions, Thomas provides the framework for what I wish to do in this second lecture. Those five questions concern:

1. The ultimate end of man.
2. The things in which man's happiness consists.
3. What is happiness?
4. What things are required for happiness?
5. The achievement of happiness.

The student of Aristotle will find in Thomas's discussion of these questions much that is familiar and much that is not.

Having argued that to be a human agent is to act deliberately for the sake of an end—and indeed, that this is peculiar to men among natural agents—Thomas asks if an act is the kind of act it is because of the end for the sake of which it is undertaken. If so, there seem to be as many ends as there are different kinds of human acts. This leads Thomas to ask whether, over and above these specific ends, there is any overriding ultimate end for the sake of which men act.[1] Having clarified what he means by such an end, Thomas asks if a person could have a plurality of ultimate ends. He argues against this possibility and then puts the most crucial question of all: Is there one and the same ultimate

1. It might be asked why the question isn't put in terms of the plurality of individual goals rather than of kinds or species of goal. The answer is that will is a rational appetite and shares in the universality that characterizes intellect. Just as mind grasps the individual as one of a kind, so will pursues a particular thing as an instance of the good. See IaIIae, q. 1, a. 2, ad 3.

end for all human agents? This opening discussion ends by asking whether earthly creatures other than man share in this ultimate end.

The *Summa theologiae* is, needless to say, a theological work. The distinction between theology and philosophy is somewhat analogous to the distinction, within philosophy, between metaphysics and the philosophy of nature. Despite the formal difference between the latter two, it is nonetheless the case that discussions from natural philosophy are subsumed into metaphysics, where they serve different ends than could be the case in their native habitat. So too, Thomas argues *both* that theology and philosophy are formally distinct *and* that philosophical doctrines are taken up by the theologian and put to work in the higher science. The favored metaphor is that the water of philosophy is transmuted into the wine of theology.[2] So that, if *in vino veritas,* the philosopher is by definition a teetotaler. In any case, he has only a watered down version of the truth.

Philosophical discussion takes place within the ambience of points of reference accessible to all. The philosopher assumes a community of discourse as wide as the race and seeks assent to conclusions on the basis of premises of which any human thinker is potentially in possession. There can be, needless to say, seemingly insuperable obstacles to communication among human beings; nonetheless, philosophical discourse is undertaken on the assumption that, whether it be reached quickly or only after agonizing dialectical exchange, there is a basis for agreement in the common nature shared by the interlocutors, a basis equally accessible to both and which neither confers on the other.

Theology, by contrast, is governed by principles accepted as true on the basis of God revealing, that is, on the basis of faith. But theological discourse, as opposed to simple faith, is a dialectical undertaking, governed by revealed truth in the way in which

2. See *In Boethii de trinitate* (ed. Decker), prooem. q. II, art. iii, ad 5: "Unde illi, qui utuntur philosophicis documentis in sacra doctrina redigendo in obsequium fidei, non miscent aquam vino, sed aquam convertunt in vinum."

philosophical discourse is governed by naturally accessible first principles.

Theology's first borrowing from philosophy can be seen in its discursive character. "Just as God, in knowing himself, knows other things in his own way, that is, by simple intuition, not discursively, so we, on the basis of the things we grasp through faith, adhering to the First Truth, come to knowledge of other things in our manner, namely, by arguing from principles to conclusions. Thus the things we hold on faith are for us as it were principles in this science and the other things are as conclusions."[3]

But it is not only methods of argumentation that theology borrows from philosophy; philosophical doctrines themselves are made use of. Indeed, theology as Thomas understands it could not come into being if philosophical doctrines were not available to it. The very first article of the *Summa theologiae* asks why, over and above the philosophical sciences, we have any need of theology.[4] Philosophy is not a necessary presupposition of faith, but it is presupposed by theology. "Similarly theology—since all other sciences are, as it were, its servants and, though inferior in dignity, preambles to it in the order in which sciences come into being—can use the principles of all the other sciences."[5]

It is no surprise, accordingly, to find that the opening five questions of the moral part of the *Summa theologiae* make such prominent use of Aristotelian philosophy. In fact, the dominant voice in these questions is that of Aristotle. This is clear first of all

3. See ibid., q. II, a. ii c.: "Et sicut deus ex hoc, quod cognoscit se, cognoscit alia modo suo, id est simplici intuitu, non discurrendo, ita nos ex his, quae per fidem capimus primae veritati adhaerendo, venimus in cognitionem aliorum secundum modum nostrum discurrendo de principiis ad conclusiones, ut sic ipsa, quae fide tenemus, sint nobis quasi principia in hic scientia et alia sint quasi conclusiones."

4. *Summa theologiae*, Ia, q. 1, a. 1.

5. "Et similiter theologia, cum omnes aliae scientiae sint huic quasi famulantes et praeambula in via generationis, quamvis sint dignitate posteriores, potest uti principiis omnium aliarum scientiarum" (*In Boethii de trinitate*, prooem. q. II, art. iii, ad 7).

on a quite material level: Aristotle is cited seventy times in the
course of these five questions, as compared with fifty-seven cita-
tions from Scripture and forty-three from Augustine. But of
course these explicit appeals do not exhaust the debt Thomas
owes Aristotle in this treatment of man's ultimate end. It is fair to
say that these discussions would have been unthinkable apart
from the influence of Aristotle, particularly, though by no means
exclusively, of his *Nicomachean Ethics.*

How is it possible for a Christian theologian to be guided in
this way by a pagan philosopher? That question becomes more
pressing when we recall the actual burden of the discussion.
Thomas is asking about the point of human life, the good for
man, the ultimate end of all human endeavor. But it was precisely
on the basis of what is now actually our ultimate end that
Jacques Maritain denied the possibility of a purely philosophical
ethics. Yet here is Thomas, in the course of treating of man's
ultimate end, relying more on Aristotle than on Scripture itself.
How is this possible?

One answer that has come into vogue is to suggest that the
Aristotle who enters into the theology of Thomas Aquinas is
not to be confused with the historical figure who wrote the
Nicomachean Ethics. Indeed, the *Nicomachean Ethics* that figures in Thomas's theological inquiries is not to be confused with
the book of the same title written by Aristotle. The truth is, we
are told, violence is being done to Aristotle in this theological use
of him: he is being measured on the Procrustean bed of an alien
discipline. It is no less an authority than Father René Antoine
Gauthier, O.P., distinguished editor of the Leonine critical editions of many of Thomas's commentaries on Aristotle, including
the commentary on the *Nicomachean Ethics,* who says such dis-
paraging things of Thomas's employment of Aristotle.[6] Thomas
thought he was changing philosophical water into theological

6. "Les responsables en sont les théologiens, notamment un Thomas d'Aquin,
précisément parce que, théologiens, ils ont dû faire violence à la sagesse grecque
pour la faire tenir dans le lit de Procuste de leur système." *Aristote L'Ethique à
Nicomaque,* introduction, trans., and commentary by R. A. Gauthier and J. Y.
Jolif, 2d ed. in 3 vol. (Louvain/Paris: Nauwaelerts, 1970, vol. 1), pp. 274–75.

wine. Gauthier accuses him of lopping off the Stagyrite's legs.[7] The suggestion is nothing less than that Thomas twists Aristotle to his own theological purposes. If this leads you to expect that Thomas will turn Aristotle into a Christian theologian, fear not. When one turns to the texts that interest us in this lecture, the opening five questions of the moral part of the *Summa,* it becomes increasingly difficult to understand why Gauthier spoke as he did. What role does Aristotle play in the questions that interest us?[8]

Aristotle in the *Summa Theologiae*

Aristotle is cited in the *sed contra est* of the first article, which seeks to establish that the end is the beginning so far as human activities go. A human act is precisely one in which we know what we are doing and freely do it. In establishing that, in the sense of the phrase "acting for an end" he is using, only man among natural agents acts for the sake of an end, Thomas is keen to show that this is compatible with Aristotle's general teleological account of natural events. Aristotle is not explicitly invoked in the argument that human acts are differentiated by the ends they pursue, but the argument depends on the preceding articles. Now Thomas arrives at the question: Is there some ultimate end of human life?

The question comes down to asking whether there is something for the sake of which other things are done but which is not itself sought for any end beyond itself. This is first clear from the objections that argue against an infinite regress. The *sed contra est* is from Aristotle: "But those who maintain the infinite series destroy the good without knowing it."[9] Why? Thomas makes the argument explicit. The good possesses the character of an end:

7. I discuss these charges of Gauthier in *Aquinas on Human Action* (Washington, D.C.: The Catholic University of America Press, 1992), pp. 169–85.

8. See Ceslao Pera, O.P., "Le Fonti del Pensiero di S. Tommaso D'Aquino nella Somma Teologica," in the *Introduzione Generale* to the Italian translation, vol. 1 (Bologna: Edizione Studio Domenicano, 1949), pp. 31–153.

9. *Metaphysics* II, 2, 994b11–12.

the good is what is sought in action and it is contrary to the notion of an end that is to be sought in an unending process. Aristotle continues the passage cited thus: "The reasonable man, at least, always acts for a purpose; and this is a limit, for the end is a limit."

That is the point Thomas seeks to establish in the body of the *Prima Secundae*, question 1, article 4, where he invokes another Aristotelian text.[10] What he has to say, if it is true, is philosophically true, true in the way Aristotle's arguments themselves must be true—that is, by appeal only to the nature of what is being discussed—in a way that is in principle adjudicable by anyone, in terms of what anyone can be expected to know. Thomas associates himself with Aristotle in the claim that a causal series cannot be infinite and that, in argumentation, there cannot be an infinite regress in the principles on which the argument depends.

It becomes clear that ultimate end as discussed thus far is, so to say, a regional principle. Thomas asked whether there is an ultimate end of human life and answered the question in such a way that a further question must still be asked: Can a person have more than one ultimate end? To this question Thomas will advance a negative answer, but he begins by presenting a number of arguments that seek to establish an affirmative answer. When the turn is made, with the *sed contra est,* all the authorities invoked are scriptural. St. Paul said of the gluttonous that "their god is the belly," meaning that they make the pleasures of eating their ultimate end. Futhermore, Our Lord said that we cannot serve two masters. Thomas takes these passages to ground the belief that a person can have only one ultimate end.

In the body of the article, Thomas gives three arguments on behalf of this. The first follows on what he takes any ultimate end to be, namely, that which is the agent's perfect and complete good. "Therefore the ultimate end must so fulfill the whole desire of man that there is nothing outside it left to desire."[11] If the

---

10. *Physics* VIII, 5, 256a17.
11. "Oportet igitur quod ultimus finis ita impleat totum hominis appetitum, quod nihil extra ipsum appetendum relinquatur. Quod esse non potest, si aliquid

ultimate end is that which leaves nothing to be desired beside itself, the same human agent can scarcely regard two things as filling the bill. The second argument draws an analogy between the process of cognition and the process of appetition, in the sense of willing. Knowledge has as its principle that which is naturally known; by analogy, appetite will have as its principle that which is naturally desired. But this must be one. Why? Because nature tends to one. He concludes that that to which the will tends as to an ultimate end must be one.

Of these two arguments, as well as of the third which follows, one would say that, if they work, they work in the way that philosophical arguments work. The wider context they require for their intelligibility is Aristotelian philosophy. That is why Thomas can invoke, in a kind of shorthand, the principle that *natura non tendit nisi ad unum*. He assumes his readers know how the truth of that is established. Thus far we have been given no theological doctrine, that is, no discourse that depends on principles accepted on the basis of divine faith. This continues to be true when Thomas asks whether an agent must will all that he wills for the sake of the ultimate end. He cites Augustine as authority for an affirmative answer, but here is the first argument he gives in the body of the article.[12]

First, because whatever a man wills, he wills as a good, and if he doesn't seek it as the perfect good, which is the ultimate end, he must seek it as tending toward the perfect good: a beginning is always ordered to the fulfillment of what is begun, something clear both in what comes about in nature and in what comes about in art. Therefore, every beginning of perfection is ordered to complete perfection, which is the ultimate end.

---

extraneum ad ipsius perfectionem requiratur. Unde non potest esse quod in duo sic tendat appetitus, ac si utrumque sit bonum perfectum ipsius" (IaIIae, q. 1, a. 5, c).

12. "Primo quidem quia quidquid homo appetit, appetit sub ratione boni. Quod quidem si non appetitur ut bonum perfectum, quod est ultimus finis, necesse est ut appetatur ut tendens in bonum perfectum; quia semper inchoatio alicuius ordinatur ad consummationem ipsius; sicut patet tam in his quae fiunt a natura, quam in his quae fiunt ab arte; Et ita omnis inchoatio perfectionis ordinatur in perfectionem consummatam, quae est per ultimum finem" (IaIIae, q. 1, a. 6, c).

The distinction crucial to this argument becomes explicit in the next article, where Thomas makes the question yet more precise by asking if there is a single ultimate end for all human agents. The foregoing would seem to provide us with the basis for a negative answer. If the glutton's belly is his god and this is his ultimate end, he will differ in this from all nongluttonous humans, and thus different agents have different ultimate ends. Yet Thomas wishes to maintain that there is a unique ultimate end for all human agents. How can he establish this?

He suggests that we notice that we can speak of ultimate end in two ways, either as the notion of ultimate end or as that object in which the ultimate end is sought. That is, the glutton and the nonglutton can be said to have the same ultimate end in the sense that both desire their complete good but they have different ultimate ends because they seek different things as their complete good. Thus, one and the same notion of ultimate end is operative when we distinguish a plurality of things in which men seek their ultimate end. If it is the case that implicit in any human action is the desire for what is fulfilling and perfecting of the agent, then all human agents, in whatever concrete things they seek, desire the complete satisfaction of rational desire.

Finally,[13] Thomas allows that everything other than God is ordered to God as to its end, yet only the rational creature orders himself to the ultimate end by knowing and loving it. This final point can be understood as a purely philosophical one, a corollary of Aristotelian teleology. If that is the case, it is clear that every point established in question one of the *Prima Secundae* is a philosophical one. If some version of the Gauthier charge were true, it would have to be true on some basis other than Thomas's heavy-handed effort to make Aristotle's teaching conform to Christian doctrine. If anything like "baptizing Aristotle" were going on in this first question, it is certainly not at the obvious level of the arguments advanced. One might still claim that the philosophical positions Thomas is here developing are different

13. Ibid., q. 1, a. 8.

from what is found in Aristotle, much as one might seek to show that there is a discrepancy between what is interpreted and the interpretation given of it in Thomas's commentary on the *Nicomachean Ethics*. Sometimes that kind of discrepancy is assumed on the same sweeping basis as Gauthier's assumption that Aristotelian doctrine is distorted by the very fact of being made use of in a theological work, and doubtless the one assumption is about as good as the other.

Question One is the establishment of a series of claims about the human agent, claims that, if they are true, are true in the way philosophical claims are. Thomas clearly thinks these claims are either identical with or derivative from Aristotelian doctrine, and I think he is right about that. What has been established, if these articles are successful, is that every human agent acts for an ultimate end, a claim that can be described as almost a formal one. The logic of action requires that any X willed is willed as a good, as having goodness; and goodness, the formality under which any X is willed, is the complete fulfillment of the agent willing. It is the value of X that interests us, accordingly. The pursuit of the ultimate end might seem to involve only that whatever is willed must be willed as at least partly fulfilling of us. Since we will now this, now that, now the other thing, but each under the formality of the good, the claim that it is part of the logic of human action that every agent seeks the ultimate end can seem to be far less adventurous than at first appeared.

God as Ultimate End

You will object that I am being disingenuous. The first question ended with the conclusion that the ultimate end of all creatures, man included, is God, but that it is man's way of attaining that end—by voluntary action—that makes him unique. Surely we have here a position peculiar to the theologian or one that bears the stamp of faith's influence on thought. In a heated passage, Gauthier makes just this point. Conceding that Thomas's procedure owes much to Aristotle, that Aristotle provides a con-

ceptual tool in making happiness the end and the end the
starting point of moral thought, Gauthier insists that this is de-
ceptive. Aristotelian ideas undergo a transformation so profound
in the use Thomas puts them to that Thomas's moral thought
becomes "the negation of the express teaching of the historical
Aristotle." [14] The words and phrases, as well as the procedure, are
the same, but the meaning is not only different from but opposed
to that of Aristotle. Gauthier illustrates what he means with
respect to the identification of the ultimate end. "The moral end,
which for Aristotle is an essentially contingent reality since it is
the action of man, is for Thomas the least contingent reality there
is, for it is God himself, not the God-object of the philosophers,
but the God-person of Christians; the end of man is not in an
action of man, not even in any action that there might be by
which he is united to God. . . ." [15]

In this passage, Father Gauthier begins by opposing what Aristotle has to say about happiness as the subjective attainment of
the end—what Thomas calls the *usus sive adeptio illius rei*—to
what Thomas has to say of the object of the attainment, *idest ipsa
res in qua ratio boni invenitur*.[16] In this way, Thomas can be
opposed to Thomas. Sensing this, doubtless anticipating the
suggestion—it is one made by Thomas—that the ultimate felicific
object for Aristotle is the divine as attained in contemplation (the
burden of Book Ten of the *Nicomachean Ethics*), Gauthier then
opposes the God of the philosophers to the God of faith. It is of
course easy to concede that Aristotle was not a Christian, but the
question is rather if and to what degree Thomas was an Aristotelian. I do not of course mean simply an allegiance to a philosophical school, but rather this: What happens to philosophical

14. "La Négation de l'enseignement exprès de l'Aristote historique"
(Gauthier, op. cit., p. 275).

15. "La fin morale, qui est pour Aristote réalité essentiellement contingente
puisqu'elle est action de l'homme, est pour saint Thomas la réalité la moins
contingente qui soit, car elle est Dieu même, non pas le dieu-objet des philoso-
phes, mais le Dieu-Personne des Chrétiens: la fin de l'homme n'est pas dans une
action de l'homme, pas même dans l'action quelle qu'elle soit par laquelle il s'unit
à Dieu . . ." (loc. cit., pp. 275–76).

16. IaIIae, q. 1, a. 8.

truths in the Christian dispensation? Are they obliterated and replaced by truths of faith and/or truths of theology? Gauthier's notion that the relationship between philosophical ethics and moral theology is one of contradictory opposition does not seem to be shared by St. Thomas Aquinas.

With What Can the Ultimate End Be Identified?

Although Thomas has identified God as the reality in whom the notion of ultimate end is perfectly realized, he devotes Question Two to establishing the negative point that human happiness cannot consist in any created good. Happiness, in the sense of the attainment of the end, what may be called subjective happiness, is of course a created attribute of a creature. But there are many things in which the human agent might seek his happiness, things in which he might think the notion of ultimate end is saved, and it is necessary to look into that. Were Thomas to settle for the claim that all men have the same ultimate end—in the sense that, no matter the radical differences in the way in which they lead their lives, the notion of ultimate end is operative in each human life—this would be weak almost to the point of vacuity. The question becomes meaty when it is asked whether there is something or some set of things in which alone the notion of ultimate end can be truly realized.

In reviewing candidates for this role—riches, honor, fame and glory, power, health, pleasure—Thomas's assessment is in terms of the agent, whose perfection is thought to consist in the attainment of such goods. These things may be constituents of the human good, but they cannot be definitive of it, man being what he is.[17] Man's soul is such that his reach lies beyond these good but insufficient objects of desire. Does his happiness then consist in some good of the soul? Thomas repeats the by-now-familiar

17. Thomas readily speaks of parts of happiness and to have a part is happiness of a sort. "Bonum autem conveniens, si quidem sit perfectum, est ipsa hominis beatitudo; si autem sit imperfectum, est quaedam beatitudinis participatio, vel propinqua vel remota, vel saltem apparens" (IaIIae, q. 2, a. 6, c).

distinction. "The thing which is desired as the end is that in which happiness consists and which makes one happy; but the attainment of this thing is called happiness. So it must be said that happiness is something of the soul, but that in which happiness consists lies outside the soul." [18]

What, then, does satisfy the notion of ultimate end? The will is an appetite consequent upon intellect, and it is the mark of intellect that it grasps the universal. The good grasped by mind, which is operative in the specification of will, is good in all its amplitude. Not this good or that, since any particular thing will be desired *sub ratione boni,* as something that is good, something that has goodness. If some particular good were identical with goodness, there would be a fusion of the formality under which anything is willed and this particular thing. And there is indeed one who is not merely good but goodness itself. Essential goodness (as opposed to participated) is a name of God. Only God saves the *ratio boni* perfectly. Only God can be man's ultimate end.

There can be no doubt that this claim, the culmination of the second question as it was of the first, sounds differently in Christian ears than it could have in pagan ears. Man is called to union with God; our destiny in the new dispensation is a beatifying vision of God; we will see even as we are seen. That this supernatural goal of human life eclipses what philosophers had to say about human happiness is so obvious that the remarks of Gauthier, to say nothing of those of Maritain and Gilson, take on an air of self-evidence. It is God attained in the beatific vision who is our ultimate end, and the capacity to achieve this state is not a natural one; only by sharing in the redeeming grace of Christ can we attain our ultimate end.

In Question Three, Thomas sets out to tell us what happiness is, and, since happiness is attained in a human activity or opera-

18. "Res ergo ipsa quae appetitur ut finis, est id in quo beatitudo consistit, et quod beatum facit: sed huius rei adeptio vocatur beatitudo. Unde dicendum est quod beatitudo est aliquid animae; sed id in quo consistit beatitudo, est aliquid extra animam" (IaIIae, q. 2, a. 7, c).

tion, the question comes down to asking in what activity happiness is achieved. Since Thomas has just argued that no created thing can be our ultimate end, he begins by repeating the distinction between the thing that is the ultimate end and the attainment, enjoyment, use, or possession of it. "In this second sense, man's ultimate end is something created, existing in him, which is nothing else but the attainment or enjoyment of the ultimate end. Considered in terms of its cause or object, man's happiness is something uncreated, but if we consider the essence of happiness, it is something created." [19]

In this context, what will Thomas make of the Aristotelian proposal that human happiness is to be found chiefly in the contemplation of the divine as this is made possible by metaphysics? Will he deny the Aristotelian claim, as Gauthier suggests, seeing it as inimical to his own properly theological conclusion that our happiness will consist in the vision of the divine essence? Surely the latter kind of attainment of God is impossible on the basis of philosophical speculation. Is the God of the philosophers opposed to the God who revealed himself in Jesus, such that to accept the latter is *eo ipso* to reject the former? The remarks of many of his followers and interpreters do not prepare us for what we actually find in Thomas Aquinas.

Let us distinguish, Thomas suggests, perfect from imperfect happiness. Perfect happiness will consist in that vision of the divine essence which is our hope; imperfect happiness is a more modest thing. The knowledge of God possible through speculative science will always fall short of attaining him as he is, in his essence. Philosophical knowledge of God is oblique, analogical— finally, knowledge of what God is not rather than what he is. Such knowledge will be constrained by its starting point in our experience of sensible reality.[20]

19. "Secundo autem modo ultimus finis hominis est aliquid creatum in ipso existens; quod nihil est aliud quam adeptio vel fruitio finis ultimi. Ultimus autem finis vocatur beatitudo. Si ergo beatitudo hominis consideretur quantum ad causam vel objectum, sic est aliquid increatum; si autem consideretur quantum ad ipsam essentiam beatitudinis, sic est aliquid creatum" (IaIIae, q. 3, a. 1, c).
20. IaIIae, q. 3, a. 6.

Now, far from simply setting aside this imperfect happiness as having been superseded in the new dispensation, Thomas begins to speak of it as the happiness that is attainable in this life. The beatific vision is not of course something attainable here below— no man has seen God and lived. Perfect happiness, accordingly, is not an end attainable in our earthly condition. This is not a remark about pagans, as opposed to Christians, but a truth about all living human agents.[21] The acknowledgment of our ultimate destiny in the vision of God, far from leading Thomas to dismiss philosophical accounts of human happiness, enables him to see them as accounts of the kind of happiness that can be attained in this world. Aristotle continues to be his guide in this regard. "If we speak of the happiness of the present life," he remarks, "then, as Aristotle says in the ninth book of the *Ethics,* the happy man needs friends."[22]

Conclusion

Thomas's interpretation of Aristotle, then, is this. The great pagan philosopher not only laid down the notion of the human good or ultimate end but went on to speak of the things in which happiness consists. The things Aristotle proposed, most notably the contemplation of God that could be based on a philosophical science, cannot really save the formality of happiness or of ultimate end, except imperfectly. By natural or philosophical knowledge we could never be aware of an attainment of God that would perfectly save the notion of happiness. But did Aristotle himself realize that what he proposed as our happiness did not fully save *his own* conception of happiness? A reiterated claim in these opening questions of the moral part of the *Summa* is that Aristotle himself recognized that what he identified as our happiness only imperfectly realized the definition of happiness he him-

21. See, for example, IaIIae, q. 4, a. 6 (". . . si loquamur de beatitudine hominis qualis in hac vita potest haberi . . .") and a. 7 (". . . ad beatitudinem imperfectam, qualis in hac vita potest haberi . . .").
22. IaIIae, q. 4, a. 8, c. "Respondeo dicendum quod, si loquamur de felicitate praesentis vitae, sicut Philosophus dicit in IX *Ethic.,* felix indiget amicis. . . ."

self set down in the *Nicomachean Ethics*. Thomas several times points to the following passage.

Why then should we not say that he is happy who is active in conformity with complete excellence and is sufficiently equipped with external goods, not for some chance period but throughout a complete life? Or must we add "and who is destined to live this and die as befits his life"? Certainly the future is obscure to us, while happiness, we claim, is an end and something in every way final. If so, we shall call blessed those among living men in whom these conditions are, and are to be, fulfilled—but blessed *men*.[23]

The account Aristotle gave of happiness—as self-sufficient, as such that, once had, it could not be lost, and so on—is of something that can be realized in this life only imperfectly. We are subject to the vagaries of chance, of health, of the economy. Massive misfortune can so alter our circumstances that our moral character is shaken and even crumbles. Aristotle is no Stoic. In any case, Thomas calls our attention to the obvious fact that Aristotle recognized that such happiness as we can attain in this life will always fall short of the ideal of happiness he set out at the opening of the *Ethics*. That continues to be true of the happiness attainable in this life—*in via*, as Thomas would say— but we, unlike Aristotle, have been given the good news that there awaits us *in patria* a happiness that perfectly saves the conception Aristotle developed.

We can therefore conclude that certain ways of describing the relationship between philosophical ethics and moral theology, far from expressing the views of Thomas, would seem to conflict with what we actually find in the *Summa theologiae*. My point does not depend on the claim that Thomas interprets Aristotle accurately, that the passages he cites from Aristotle in the course of these opening questions have exactly the meaning he takes them to have, or even that he is historically and textually right

23. *Nicomachean Ethics* I, 10, 1101a14–21. Thomas cites this passage in IaIIae, q. 3, a. 2, and in q. 5, a. 2; in a number of other places he notes the discrepancy between happiness as Aristotle defined it and what is attainable in this life. See q. 2, a. 4; q. 4, a. 6; q. 5, a. 3.

that Aristotle recognized that any happiness attainable in this life falls short of the ideal of happiness Aristotle described. There are solid reasons for being confident in Thomas as an exegete of Aristotle and for accepting what he has to say about Aristotle's recognition that there is a gap between what we aspire to and what we can attain in the matter of happiness. But waiving all that, there would remain the fact that Thomas himself constructs, in the course of doing moral theology, arguments that, if they are sound, are so on the basis of principles accessible to nonbeliever as well as believer. That is, it is possible to formulate true practical guidelines as to how in this life happiness can be achieved, and the truth of such precepts is independent of the truths that are held to be such only on the basis of divine faith.

Moral theology is not a Procrustean bed on which philosophical doctrine is mutilated. Rather, theology is the upper berth, philosophy the lower and without a foot on the latter you will never get to the former.

CHAPTER III

The Role of Faith in Moral Philosophizing

These lectures have as their overarching theme the relationship between faith and morals. There are some, as we have seen, who would reduce Christianity to a morality without remainder: it is just an ethics and nothing else; moreover, it is an ethics that can be completely separated from the historical accidents and mythical overlay of the Christian story. In order to be an ethics, a doctrine has to submit itself to human reason unadorned by faith, and if it cannot withstand such rational scrutiny it must be consigned to the dustbin of history. The only ethics there is, is philosophical ethics. (Something like this is the target of Søren Kierkegaard's *Philosophical Fragments*.)

Diametrically opposed to this are those who hold that the only adequate ethics is a Christian ethics. Sometimes this is a special case of the general claim that the only adequate philosophy is Christian philosophy, but often it is an argument about practical, moral knowledge alone. Given the objective of moral knowledge to direct concrete choices here and now, an ethics whose precepts are not an ordering of the agent to the ultimate end of the beatific vision will be inadequate to the human agent in his present historical actuality.

Etienne Gilson and Jacques Maritain were Thomists, indeed leaders of the Thomistic revival. Their strong views on the limits of philosophical ethics are put forward in part as accounts, in part as developments of what they have learned from Thomas Aquinas. It is just this that produces something of a surprise. Gilson and Maritain, to say nothing of Gauthier, are, not to put too fine a point upon it, stingy in their praise of the Stagyrite. They depict the moral teaching of Thomas as palpably different from that of Aristotle, different in the way in which Christianity differs from paganism. Nor is it merely a matter of going beyond Aristotle. Gauthier at least argues that there is opposition between Aristotelian and Thomistic ethics, that the latter negates the former. (His essay on Thomas and the *Ethics* of Aristotle, appended to the Leonine edition of Thomas's commentary on the *Politics,* does not really take back Gauthier's earlier excessive statements.) Nonetheless, when we read Thomas himself, evidence of this split is hard to come by. On the contrary, Thomas's moral theology begins more obviously under the guidance of Aristotle than under that of sacred Scripture and the Christian tradition. It is inescapable that Thomas sees a continuing truth in Aristotelian ethics, one that has not been negated by Christian revelation. Indeed, as is generally the case with theology as Thomas understands it, without moral philosophy there could be no moral theology.

In this lecture I shall attempt to push the argument forward by addressing a number of further issues. First, I will propose that the analogy of the *praeambula fidei,* which Maritain rejected, ought rather to be accepted and its implications drawn. That is, Maritain, stressing the difference between speculative and practical reason, allowed that natural reason can arrive at some knowledge of God (*praeambula fidei*), yet denied that there can be adequate natural knowledge of morality independent of faith. Second, I will dwell on what would seem to follow if some versions of the Christian philosophy view is maintained, namely, that Thomas's teaching on natural law would have to be jettisoned. Third, I will infer from what has been said a conception of Christian philosophy that does not have the unhappy consequences some other expressions of the notion seem to me to have.

Praeambula Fidei

When Jacques Maritain developed his conception of moral philosophy adequately considered, he was careful to confine the inadequacy of philosophy to morals, to practical reason. "Yet, again, be careful to avoid confounding the character of speculative science with that of practical science. Theodicy does not give a sufficient knowledge of God as He is in the mystery of the Deity, yet it is sufficient for a knowledge of God as Cause of being: but an independent moral philosophy is essentially incompetent in regard to the proper object of moral science."[1] Whatever Maritain has to say of the inadequacy of philosophy, of its necessary subalternation to theology, is to be understood as applying to moral philosophy alone. Practical reason and practical science differ from theoretical reason and theoretical science. Gilson may suggest that it is only under the influence of Exodus that a true or adequate metaphysics can be constructed, but Maritain proceeds more carefully. In the passage just quoted, he reminds us that natural theology—he calls it theodicy here—is possible. I suggest that we look at the way Thomas related that possibility to the faith and then ask whether we must, as Maritain suggests, reject anything analogous to this in the moral order.

In a famous passage in the *Summa contra gentes*,[2] Thomas observes that there are two kinds of truth about God, those which can be arrived at by the use of unaided natural reason, and those which God has deigned to reveal. If God had not revealed it to mankind, we would not know that there are three persons in the Trinity, that Jesus is human and divine, that sins are forgiven by Christ's redemptive sacrifice, and so on. Almost any article of

1. Jacques Maritain, *Science and Wisdom,* trans. Bernard Wall (London: Geoffrey Bles, 1944), pp. 165–66.
2. I, 3: "Est autem in his quae de Deo confitemur duplex veritatis modus. Quaedam namque vera sunt de Deo quae omnem facultatem humanae rationis excedunt, ut Deum esse trinum et unum. Quaedam vero sunt ad quae etiam ratio naturalis pertingere potest, sicut est Deum esse, Deum esse unum, et alia huiusmodi; quae etiam philosophi demonstrative de Deo probaverunt, ducti naturalis lumine rationis."

the Nicene Creed would illustrate the point. If we are asked why we hold the truth of the Trinity, our answer must be because God has revealed it. Such truths about God, Thomas calls mysteries of faith.

As opposed to what? There are some truths about God that can be grounded in what everyone, believer or not, knows—truths such as that God exists, that there is only one God, that everything other than God depends on him in order to be, and so on. If Thomas is a lot clearer on this distinction than his predecessors, this is because of historical factors we mentioned in the first lecture. St. Paul's statement that the Romans' misbehavior, which he chronicles, was inexcusable because they could "from the things that are made, come to knowledge of the invisible things of God" was from the beginning recognized as saying that pagans can arrive at knowledge of God from their knowledge of the things of this world.[3] Thomas, living at the time when the *Physics* and *Metaphysics* of Aristotle became available in the West, was able to compile quite a list of such truths about God that philosophers had acquired.

The distinction suggests that we can form two lists of truths about God. The first will contain those which can be decided on the basis of what anyone knows; the second will contain truths held to be such only on the authority of revelation. The first set falls to philosophical theology, the culminating effort of metaphysics and indeed of all philosophy as Aristotle and Plato envisaged it; the second set is to be found in revelation, in the Scriptures.

It is the second set of truths that Thomas calls the principles of theology. The theologian differs from other believers in this: that, in reflecting on revealed truths, he draws out their implications, compares them with one another, and defends them against attack. But his discipline, as one distinct from philosophy, depends on the truth of principles that are held to be true on the basis of faith in revelation.

3. If such knowledge of God as is possible to pagans counts as speculative science, it is clear that Paul thinks it has practical significance as well. If God exists, then not everything is permitted.

This raises a problem. If we were to equate what has been revealed about God with mysteries of faith, that is, with truths that can be accepted only on the basis of God's authority, we would face a difficulty when we noticed that truths about God of the first sort seem contained in Scripture, too. That God exists, that there is but one God, that he is intelligent, that he causes other things to be—all these deliverances of natural theology seem part of revelation. How could the believer believe other truths about God if he did not hold that God exists? The Trinity poses special difficulties, because the believer holds that there is only one God. And so on. What seemed like a clean distinction into two non-overlapping lists, appears to blur and the lists to coalesce. The truths that philosophers came to know have been proposed for our belief in revelation. Either all truths about God are mysteries of faith or not everything that has been revealed need be accepted on the basis of faith.

Thomas takes the second tack. If he took the first he would be committed to this: there are truths about God that can be known, and these same truths can be held to be such only on the basis of revelation. Under the pressure of such considerations, Thomas began to speak of *praeambula fidei*.[4] Among the things that God has revealed are some truths about himself that are knowable by natural reason. These are as it were preambles to those revealed truths which cannot in this life be known to be true, the *mysteria fidei*. The preambles are included in revelation, not because it is necessary that they be believed, but because they are presupposed by the mysteries and also because, for those who do not have knowledge of them, they can be accepted on faith.[5]

---

4. ". . . dicendum quod Deum esse, et alia huiusmodi quae per rationem naturalem nota possunt esse de Deo, ut dicitur Rom. 1,19, non sunt articuli fidei, sed praeambula ad articulos: sic enim fides praesupponit cognitionem naturalem, sicut gratia naturam, et perfectio perfectibile. Nihil tamen prohibet illud quod secundum se demonstrabile est et scibile, ab aliquo accipi ut credibile, qui demonstrationem non capit" (Ia, q. 2, a. 2, ad 1).

5. ". . . ea quae demonstrative probari possunt inter credenda numerantur, non quia de ipsis simpliciter sit fides apud omnes: sed quia praeexiguntur ad ea quae sunt fidei, et oportet ea saltem per fidem praesupponi ab his qui eorum demonstrationem non habent" (IIaIIae, q. 1, a. 5, ad 3).

An Analogue in Practical Reason

Truths about God of either sort distinguished by Thomas would fall to the theoretical or speculative intellect, but they are truths which some few men, with much effort and with admixture of error, would arrive at in the evening of their lives. The truths about God Thomas calls preambles of faith are, when known, conclusions, but conclusions remote from the starting points of reasoning. Indeed, among the reasons Thomas regularly cites for the fittingness of such in-principle-knowable truths being revealed is precisely the fact that they are extremely difficult to arrive at, yet they are such that postponing certainty about them until late in life would deprive them of the influence they should have. It matters a good deal as to how I will live whether or not there is a God.

There is an important parallel in practical reason to the preambles of faith in speculative reason. Among the things God has revealed are precepts meant to guide our actions, notably those of the Decalogue. Thomas discusses the Ten Commandments in those questions of the *Prima Secundae* that have come to be called the Treatise on Law.[6] "Law" is an analogous term for Thomas, the most obvious and controlling meaning of which is civil law. When he defines law as nothing other than a promulgated rational ordering to the common good on the part of the one who has charge of the community, we think, as we are meant to, of monarchs or bodies of lawmakers and the like.[7] The term is extended from this use to mean the eternal law by which God governs his creation, the divine law and the natural law. In an ontological sense (*secundum rem nominis*), the primary law is eternal law, but the primary analogate, that with reference to

6. The treatise begins with q. 90 and continues through the discussion of the divine law, old and new, ending with q. 108.

7. The four articles of IaIIae, q. 90, provide the elements of the definition of law given in article 4: "Et sic ex quatuor praedictis potest colligi definitio legis, quae nihil est aliud quam quaedam rationis ordinatio ad bonum commune, ab eo qui curam communitatis habet, promulgata."

which we see why the others are called law, is the civil law (*ratio propria nominis*).[8]

One of the senses of law that has drawn much attention to these questions of St. Thomas is natural law. All creatures are governed by the eternal law, the divine providence, but the rational creature shares in this governance in a special way, providing for himself and others. Thanks to this special way of sharing in eternal law, man has a natural inclination to do what he ought to do and toward his end.[9]

When the Psalmist said "Sacrifice the sacrifice of justice," as if responding to those asking what the works of justice are, he adds, "Many ask who will show us the good?" and to this he answers, "The light of thy countenance is sealed upon us, O Lord," as if the natural light of reason whereby we discern what is good and what evil, which pertain to natural law, is nothing else than the impress of the divine light on us. Thus it is evident that natural law is simply the rational creature's participation in eternal law.

Later, Thomas will identify natural law with the first precepts of practical reason, the non-gainsayable truths that mark the limits of moral discourse. These common and naturally (as opposed to discursively) known first principles, are latent or implicit in particular moral judgments that are discursively arrived at. These principles are thus said to preside over moral philosophy in general—over ethics, domestic governance, political action, and of course the civil law.

8. The term "law" has as its controlling meaning "civil law" and is then extended to Providence as the law whereby God governs creation, i.e. eternal law. If eternal law is called "law" only derivatively, nonetheless that which is most properly called law, civil law, would not have been were it not for eternal law. It is a commonplace of Thomas's doctrine on divine names that while the names shared by God and creature are such that it is the creature who lays first claim to them, nonetheless, the reality the term signifies as said of God is ontologically prior to created reality. And this in turn is an instance of the Aristotelian principle that what is most easily known by us is ontologically least perfect, and vice versa.

9. "Unde cum Psalmista dixisset (4,6), *Sacrificate sacrificium iustitiae*, quasi quibusdam quaerentibus quae sunt iustitiae opera, subiungit: *Multi dicunt quis ostendit nobis bona?* cui quaestioni respondens, dicit: *Signatum est super nos lumen vultus tui, Domine:* quasi lumen rationis naturalis, quo discernimus quid sit bonum et quid malum, quod pertinet ad naturalem legem, nihil aliud sit quam impressio divini luminis in nobis. Unde patet quod lex naturalis nihil aliud est quam participatio legis aeternae in rationali creatura" (IaIIae, q. 91, a. 2).

I remind you of these familiar matters only with an eye to drawing attention to what Thomas has to say of the relation of divine law to natural law, more particularly of the relation of the Old Law to natural law. The Law was given to the Jews as to the chosen people. God did not become everyman or any man, he became incarnate as a Jew, and special attention was shown by God to the people from which the Messiah would come.[10] Since the Law was given to the Jews, the question arises as to whether all men are bound by it. Thomas offers a qualified Yes to this question, replying that "the Old Law manifested precepts of natural law, to which it added a number of special precepts. Consequently, with respect to that of natural law that the Old Law contains, all were held to the observance of the Old Law, not because they were [precepts] of the Old Law, but because they pertain to natural law."[11]

We are being told that the Old Law contained not only precepts peculiar to the chosen people (in order that they might as a people fulfill their providential role), but also precepts of natural law. Moral precepts are practical judgments of fitting or unfitting ways to act: good acts are those in accord with reason, evil acts those discordant with reason. Just as there are first common principles, which govern speculative reason, so there are first naturally known principles, which govern all judgments of practical reason. Some things about human acts are so obvious that they can be approved or rejected right off, after the slightest consideration; judgments about other acts require intense inquiry into their different circumstances, and not everyone is equipped for such inquiry; yet other things are such that man needs the help of divine instruction in order to judge, as in matters of faith.[12] On the basis of the cadenza, Thomas can say that

10. IaIIae, q. 98, a. 4.
11. "Respondeo dicendum quod lex vetus manifestabat praecepta legis naturae, et superaddebat quaedam propria praecepta. Quantum igitur ad illa quae lex vetus continebat de lege naturae, omnes tenebantur ad observantiam verteris legis; non quia erant de veteri lege, sed quia erant de lege naturae" (IaIIae, q. 98, a. 5, c; see as well q. 100, a. 1).
12. I am paraphrasing IaIIae, q. 100, a. 1.

while all moral precepts pertain to natural law, they do so in different ways. Those acts reason grasps straightaway as to be done or avoided pertain absolutely to natural law. What are some examples? "Honor thy father and mother." "Do not kill." In short, precepts of the Decalogue are said to be unqualifiedly precepts of natural law.[13] Other moral precepts are arrived at discursively from natural law precepts, and pertain to natural law only in that sense, as derived from it.

Precepts of the Decalogue pertain to natural law. Natural law consists of precepts that no one can fail to know, the starting points of practical reasoning. Thomas even speaks of them as self-evident. The implication is astounding. Self-evident principles of practical reason have been revealed, are part of Revelation, of divine law, specifically, the Old Law. God gave the tables of the Law to Moses. We are bound to be reminded of what Thomas called *praeambula fidei*. If the connection should escape us, it is explicitly brought to our attention. Sinful practice can obscure both the common moral precepts as well as more particular ones, and that is why it is fitting that they be underwritten by the authority of divine law.[14]

Among the things proposed for our belief are not only those which reason cannot attain, such as that God is triune, but also those which right reason can grasp, such as that God is one, for the exclusion of human reason's error, which occurs in many.

The parallel, then, is clear. Just as truths about God that can be naturally known are nonetheless revealed because of the difficulty of acquiring such knowledge, so the most common rules of action, those that are said to be self-evident, non-gainsayable, are revealed. In the latter case the reason is not the intrinsic difficulty

13. "Quaedam enim sunt quae statim per se ratio naturalis cuiuslibet hominis diiudicat esse facienda vel non facienda: sicut *Honora patrem tuum et matrem tuam,* et *Non occides, Non furtum facies.* Et huiusmodi sunt absolute de lege naturae" (IaIIae, q. 100, a. 1).

14. "Sicut etiam inter credenda nobis proponuntur non solum ea ad quae ratio attingere non potest, ut Deum esse trinum; sed etiam ea ad quae ratio recta pertingere potest, ut Deum esse unum; ad excludendum rationis humanae errorem, qui accidebat in multis" (IaIIae, q. 99, a. 2, ad 2).

of the principles but rather that moral misbehavior clouds the mind and can cause confusion about all but the most general precepts of all, such as that good ought to be done and evil avoided. If in the first case, revelation is an expedient, in the second it is a remedy.

Christian Philosophy

The notion of preambles of faith enables us to give an obviously noncontroversial sense to the phrase "Christian philosophy." The Christian philosopher, thanks to his faith, has a certitude that shares in the certitude of faith about some naturally knowable truths. Indeed, on the basis of Romans 1.19, the believer believes that it is possible apart from faith to arrive at knowledge of God. Paul is suggesting, we remember, that there are moral implications of such knowledge, and this raises a question to which we shall turn in a moment: Is knowledge of moral truths dependent upon knowledge of God? But for the nonce, it is the way in which the *praeambula fidei* save one of Gilson's accounts of Christian philosophy that I wish to emphasize.

Gilson mentioned some philosophical truths that have for their first habitat revelation, those things the believer accepts on the authority of God revealing. Thomas's doctrine of *praeambula fidei* says exactly that. And Gilson (good historian that he was) wished to underscore that as an historical fact, a fact about how philosophy actually developed.[15] It can be added that, quite apart from truths about God and common moral principles, Christianity provided the occasion for acquiring clarity as to the notions of person and nature, of relation, of separated substances. Our understanding of time has undoubtedly been sharpened; so also our understanding of other durations, eviternity and eternity. One could go on. Any number of philosophical achievements would have been inconceivable apart from the Christian belief of the thinkers who made them. And it is equally easy to

15. See Lecture I above.

concede that such philosophical clarifications were often made within theology when theologians felt the need of more than existing philsophy could supply. The controversy about Christian philosophy should not, then, bear on these matters. Indeed, it is difficult to imagine anyone denying them. The dispute may be seen to turn rather on the continuing role of Christian faith in the holding of such philosophical acquisitions. Would anyone seriously object to the contention that, though some philosophical truths were discovered by Christians guided by their faith, these truths as philosophical, once acquired, depend only on the philosophical principles needed to sustain them? Sometimes Gilson seems to suggest this. Indeed, part of Gilson's dispute with Van Steenberghen turned on whether such philosophical contributions within theology could be separated out and called collectively the philosophy of St. Bonaventure, say.[16] Gilson's point was that they could not survive as separated from the place of their origin.

This claim is in many ways more plausible in the case of Bonaventure than in the case of Thomas. Bonaventure has much to say about philosophy, but we have from him no vision of the development of philosophy in individual disciplines and as a whole. The case with Aquinas is otherwise. Not only do we have a clear notion as to what he took philosophy and its constitutive sciences to be; he made contributions in almost all areas of philosophy, if only via his commentaries on Aristotle. Father Chenu, speaking of these commentaries, observes how Thomas as commentator engages in the very intellectual effort he is commenting on.[17] His is an effort to assimilate the philosophical science in question. If then we find, as we do, all kinds of philosophical achievements, clarifications, and arguments in the theological works of Thomas, and if we take them out of their theological context, we have a place to put them. We can see them as Thomas's contribu-

16. See Fernand van Steenberghen, *La philosophie au XIIIe siècle* (Louvain, 1966).
17. M.-D. Chenu, O.P., *Introduction à l'étude de Saint Thomas D'Aquin* (Paris: Vrin, 1954), pp. 173–98.

tions to the philosophical sciences he first encounters in Aristotle. It is this same Aristotelian philosophical base that enables him to absorb contributions of Neoplatonists. The reader of Thomas's commentary on the *Liber de causis,* a book anonymously fashioned from the *Elements of Theology* of Proclus, must be struck by the constant presence of Aristotle. (One might consult the *index nominum* of either the Saffrey or the Pera edition.)[18] It is clear that Thomas appraises, accepts or rejects, Proclus on the basis of the compatibility of his teachings with what he has already learned from Aristotle. It is of course absurd to equate the philosophy of Thomas with that of Aristotle; but it is worse than absurd to try to turn Thomas into a Platonist. The platonism we find in Thomas is there on condition of its being grafted onto a science Aristotelian in its origin.

Maritain's claim that moral philosophy, in order to be an adequate guide to the human agent as he actually exists, must be subalternated to theology is the most serious obstacle in the path of the claim that there is a purely philosophical ethics. Maritain's position, we remember, had to do with the fact that man is called to a supernatural end and that, even if he can still be said to have a natural end, he cannot effectively pursue his natural end unless he is also pursuing his supernatural end. This is taken to mean that when the moral philosopher fashions precepts with an eye to the natural end, these precepts would mislead rather than guide the agent.

This seems quite wrong. Maritain himself notes that Aristotelian ethics enables us to formulate such precepts as "do not steal," " do not lie," and the like. In what is their inadequacy to be seen? It is of course obvious that no action performed in conformity with such a rule of justice would be meritorious of salvation, however good an act it might be.

18. *Sancti Thomae de Aquino Super Librum De Causis Expositio,* ed. H. D. Saffrey, O.P. (Fribourg: Société Philosophique, 1954), p. 146, or *S. Thomae Aquinatis in Librum De Causis Expositio,* ed. Ceslao Pera, O.P. (Turin: Marietti, 1955), p. 152.

It might be maintained that, however good of its kind an act performed in conformity with such a precept would be, man in his sinful condition is incapable of bringing off a good act, and that only in the state of grace can he perform naturally good acts as well as meritorious acts. That would sound to me a lot more like universal depravity than anything I recognize as a Catholic conception of the effects of original sin. Granted that the will is more severely affected than the intellect, it seems excessive to say that sinful man is wholly incapable of a naturally good action— that is, one in conformity with such moral precepts as are fashioned in pagan ethics.[19] How, one might wonder, could Paul describe the antics of the Romans as inexcusable if they were incapable of acting otherwise than they did. *Non enim nobis praecipitur impossibile.*[20] If there is a law inscribed in men's hearts, a law made up of precepts, and we are wholly incapable of acting in accord with them, nature would be in vain.

If it is granted that philosophical ethics can give true advice as to how man, naturally considered, can act well, that would seem to be a more than sufficient basis for the claim that a philosophical ethics is possible—possible because it is actual. *Ab esse ad posse valet illatio.*

To object that a philosophical ethics is defective because it does not as such bring it about that men act well, would be to demand of moral science far more than Thomas himself does. The same objection could of course be brought against moral theology. The fixed dispositions that assure good action are called virtues rather than sciences; the kind of practical knowl-

---

19. This is, of course, a vast subject. See *Summa theologiae,* Ia, q. 109, aa. 1 & 2. The strength of Maritain's position lies in the fact that, without grace, the human agent is incapable of meritorious action. This has to do with man's supernatural end; grace is also needed for the healing of nature due to sin. If the adequacy of a moral theory were taken to depend upon its assuring good action on the part of those who accept it, this would seem to be a demand that a moral theory be true with practical truth. But St. Thomas distinguishes practical truth from the truth with which moral philosophy or theology are true. See *Summa theologiae,* Ia, q. 1, a. 6, ad 3, and IaIIae, q. 57, a. 5, ad 3.

20. *In Boethii de trinitate,* prooem. q. I, a. ii, sed contra 3.

edge that is a proximate guide of action is prudence. In an important passage, Thomas distinguishes the different practical sciences from the types of prudence that correspond to them.[21]

The Specter of Fideism

Is it not clear that a fundamental reason for the Church's long and sometimes lonely defense of natural law is precisely to insure that communication is possible between believers and nonbelievers? Who has not been struck by the way magisterial teaching on moral matters regularly proceeds on two levels, that of natural law and that of the Gospels. The first level engages every human agent, the second connects only with believers. The togetherness of the two in such documents should not lead us to believe that the same presuppositions are present in both cases. But it is not only critics of the magisterium who make this confusion—calling natural law arguments against homosexuality, contraception, and abortion Catholic—some dissenting theologians do the same. One often hears it said that natural law is a theological doctrine. There is a sense of this that is eminently true, but the suggestion seems not to be that we can find theological accounts of natural law, but that an acceptance of the contents of natural law depends upon religious faith. If this were the case, it would render natural law nonsensical, certainly in the uses to which the Church puts it in such documents as *Humanae vitae, Donum vitae,* and the like.[22]

There is of course a paradox here and one worth reflecting on. Whatever the claims as to the accessibility by natural reason of basic truths about action, the Church can seem to be almost alone in asserting the range of natural reason. If contraception is a violation of natural law, that is, a deed that anyone ought to see as morally defective on the basis of natural knowledge of who

---

21. *In VI Ethicorum Aristotelis,* lect. 7, n. 1200 (= *Sententia Libri Ethicorum* VI, 7, ll. 87–102).
22. See Janet E. Smith, *Humanae Vitae, A Generation Later* (Washington, D.C.: The Catholic University of America Press, 1992).

and what we are and what our good is, an awful lot of people seem unaware of it—indeed, are outrightly hostile to it. It can seem to us that, apart from the Church's, there is no voice being raised on behalf of fundamental truths about human action. We do not await congressional resolutions on such matters, we do not expect the United Nations or the World Court to issue such reminders. No wonder strictures on contraception and homosexuality and abortion are considered peculiarly Catholic and the Church's teaching is taken to be an effort to impose on people not of her confession rules of merely intramural range. Of course, the Church is the custodian of the natural law as well as of divine law, but not in such a way as to blur the distinction between the two. That the Church should now be the chief, almost sole, defender of the range of reason, theoretical and practical, has its ironies when one remembers the inflated hopes with which the modern era began. The paradox of the human need for a divine sanction for the natural is simply a continuation of the paradox of the Decalogue. In the Decalogue, if Thomas is right, we have natural law precepts receiving a divine sanction in the Mosaic Law. The need for this was caused by the darkness due to sin. Disordered appetites twist the mind from truths it should know straightaway. This makes it clear that we can, by our mode of life, render ourselves all but incapable of recognizing the obvious in the moral order.

It is not part of the doctrine of natural law that any and every human agent, no matter the moral quality of his life, can straight off and without trouble grasp as true such precepts as those of the Decalogue, even though these principles present no difficulty to the mind of one pursuing the good.

CHAPTER IV

Faith, Philosophy, and Theology

The first of these lectures drew attention to the remarkable fact that two of the most eminent Thomists of our time held a view on the status of moral philosophy, of philosophical ethics, that must function as either an obstacle or an opportunity for anyone who thinks that philosophy, including ethics, retains its distinctive character even in the ages of faith. The second lecture suggested that Thomas himself did not share the misgivings of some of his followers about natural morality. His use of Aristotle at the beginning of the moral part of the *Summa theologiae,* far from being the distorting exploitation Father Gauthier would have us believe, represents a rearguing of Aristotelian themes. That such a natural ethics is not opposed to the faith is clear, Thomas suggests, from the fact that Aristotle himself recognized that the happiness we can attain in this life is imperfect and does not measure up to the ideal of happiness Aristotle himself had spelled out.

The third lecture argued for various ways in which moral philosophy, despite its formal difference from moral theology and its intrinsic independence of the faith, benefits from the faith of the Christian philosopher as well as from the Church's role in interpreting both the natural moral law and the Gospel message. This final lecture could be described as an effort to show how moral theology benefits from moral philosophy.

Theology and Philosophy

Mention has already been made of Thomas's view that, in the order of learning, theology comes after philosophy. We saw that, at the outset of the *Summa theologiae,* he actually asks if there is need for any discipline beyond those already acquired in the study of philosophy. No one can read that Thomistic masterpiece without encountering again and again its assumption that the reader is already acquainted with the philosophy of Aristotle. But if the study of philosophy antedates the study of theology, faith, in those fortunate enough to have it, antedates them both. The believer's motivation in undertaking the study of philosophy should be considerably different from that of the nonbeliever. Moreover, he will be guided from the outset by the magisterium of the Church, not least in his choice of a mentor and guide. One of the inestimable blessings of the believing philosopher is that he is guided by the reiterated judgment of the Church that, in matters philosophical as well as theological, there is no master who can equal St. Thomas Aquinas. Whatever the personal and institutional deficiencies in past efforts to make Thomism an effective force in the contemporary quest for truth, that task remains the most urgent one confronting us. In modern times, from 1879 and *Aeterni Patris* through Vatican II documents on education and on the training of priests, the message has been the same. *Ite ad thomam.*

There have been those who object that such a sanction for a particular philosophy is an intrusion into the freedom of choice we should have in this matter. A moment's reflection will bring the realization that our choice at the outset of study is not whether or not we shall follow advice, but what and whose advice we will follow. All too often Catholics wander into philosophy under the guidance of those who accept views not only questionable in themselves but in conflict with the faith. It is in any case nonsense to imagine an initiation into philosophy that does not involve dependence on the advice of others, on college catalogues, on the categories of booksellers, on pure chance.[1] Enlightenment efforts to clear the intellectual landscape in pursuit of an absolute starting point for philosophy failed one after the other, as the Kierkegaard who wrote the unfinished story *Johannes Climacus; or De omnibus dubitandum est* knew they would.[2]

Cardinal Newman did not find it paradoxical that the exercise of natural reason should be sustained and supported by the teaching Church. In the magnificent final chapter of the *Apologia pro vita sua,* we read this:

And thus I am brought to speak of the Church's infallibility, as a provision, adapted by the mercy of the Creator, to preserve religion in the world, and to restrain that freedom of thought, which of course in itself is one of the greatest of our natural gifts, and to rescue it from its own suicidal excesses. And let it be observed that, neither here nor in what follows, shall I have occasion to speak directly of Revelation in its subject-matter, but in reference to the sanction which it gives to truths which may be known independently of it—as it bears upon the defence of natural religion.[3]

By natural religion Newman can be taken to mean, among other things, the results of the effort that came to be called philosophical theology. He saw the Church as the custodian of the natural as well as of the supernatural, of reason as well as of faith.

The theologian brings to bear on what has been revealed whatever in the preambulatory sciences of philosophy is relevant to his task of clarifying, defending, and drawing out the further implications of what God has revealed. In our times, of course, philosophy is thought of as a special discipline among others, but a Thomas *redivivus* would I think say that by "philosophy" should be meant whatever knowledge men can attain by their

1. See my *Thomism in an Age of Renewal,* Doubleday, New York, 1966, reissued in paperback by the University of Notre Dame Press in 1968. While the context in which this book was written, and its optimism, seem distant now, it contains a thought or two of pertinence still.

2. Søren Kierkegaard, *Johannes Climacus; or, De omnibus dubitandum est,* trans. T. H. Croxall (Stanford: Stanford University Press, 1958).

3. John Henry Cardinal Newman, *Apologia pro vita sua,* ed. David J. DeLaura (New York: Norton Critical Editions, 1968), p. 189.

natural powers: philosophy, history, the social sciences, the arts and, needless to say, the hard sciences. Theology is not called the Queen of the Sciences in order to give one specialist an advantage over other specialists. Indeed, the task of the theologian is so broad and deep we may wonder if any one person can bring it off even imperfectly. The humanist's slogan, that he considers nothing human alien to him, sounds almost restrictive alongside the catholicity of interest that in principle is asked of the theologian.

The task of the theologian is an ecclesial one—he does his work for the sake of the Church and within the supporting ambience of the magisterium. The recent *Instruction on the Ecclesial Vocation of the Theologian*[4] is a welcome restatement of this for any who have been tempted to think of the theologian as a freebooter, perhaps as an ombudsman, protecting the laity from the messages of the magisterium. A mere philosopher may be annoyed by the suggestion of some that philosophers provide just so many languages or points of view that the theologian can employ. This of course is to embrace a radical relativism, a subjective account of knowledge. It is perhaps here more than any other place, in its flatfooted solid realism, that Thomistic philosophy can be most at the service of theology. It is often observed that most of the current confusions in theology are traceable to philosophical mistakes.

You will of course be thinking that such an overview of philosophizing, such guidance as takes into account the possible service or disservice philosophy can be to the faith, is precisely the vantagepoint of the faith. The tyro who responds to the magisterium in these matters is acting qua believer and what he responds to is a comprehensive vision embracing the range and uses of natural reason. The believer who follows the advice of the magisterium and takes Thomas as his chief guide in philosophy has a certainty that participates in the certainty of faith that he is on the right path. This will of course have its effect when difficulties arise. As a learner he will be docile with a docility that relates him to the magisterium as well as to the page and discussion before him.

4. Congregation for the Doctrine of the Faith, Vatican City, May 24, 1990.

The vantagepoint from which philosophy and philosophizing are related beyond themselves to the great fund of truths that God has revealed is not a philosophical one. It is the teaching Church and the theologian as the servant of the teaching Church who speak of these relations. Just so, when we read of *praeambula fidei,* truths that have de facto been revealed but are in principle knowable and thus need not be believed, we know we are reading theology. Only the theologian has the competence to distinguish among revealed truths those which are mysteries of faith and those which are preambles of faith. And there are several connected issues that it falls to the theologian to consider.

He will ask why it is that God has revealed to us truths that we can learn on our own.

He will ask if we should accept on faith only those truths we can subsequently come to know to be true.

He will wonder whether it is not frivolous to accept as true what we cannot know to be true.

He will ask whether the truths of faith can conflict with what we know to be true.

He will ask whether it is wise to fashion arguments about mysteries of faith, given that these can never be decisive as to the truth of the mysteries.

These are of course the preliminary considerations with which Book One of the *Summa Contra Gentes* begins. Only the theologian can ask such questions with profit, and what he has to say will have important effects on the context—the existential context, we are perhaps likely to say—in which philosophizing is done. We will learn from him what enormous advantages reason derives from the faith. The most obvious and important is a confidence in what Jacques Maritain called the range of reason. Can we arrive at definitive knowledge that the soul survives death? Can we arrive at knowledge that God exists and learn something of what he is like from our knowledge of the things of this world? Are there moral absolutes that can be grasped by the human mind independently of the influence of faith?[5]

Put these questions to the vast majority of philosophers today and the answer you receive would be negative—the negative coming after initial befuddlement that such questions are actually being asked. It is the Church that, as Newman saw, is the great defender of the natural and the human. It is the Church that will defend reason against the betrayal of reason's supposed custodians, the philosophers. And, more pertinently to the topic of these lectures, it is the Church—and it often seems only the Church—that comes to the defense of the natural moral law.

Let me underscore the paradox. It is natural reason that is capable of arriving at truth on these matters—the immortality of the soul, the existence and nature of God, the great moral truths, which define the practical order: these are precisely achievements of philosophy. But to dub them *praeambula fidei* is to look at them in a theological perspective. The magisterium and the theologian of course recognize that, if the correct philosophical answers to those questions were taken to be in the negative—death is the end for human persons, there is no transcendent entity of the kind men call God, in morals there are no nongainsayble principles—if such negative positions were taken to be true, they would be devastating for the faith. That is precisely why the Church cannot be indifferent to natural reason and must advise the faithful in matters of philosophy as well as theology.

But what is the theologian's competence in these matters? If philosophers reach negative conclusions, what business is it of his? Because the theologian takes the principles of his inquiry from his faith, he knows that the clear sense of Revelation is that God can be known in this life from his effects, known even by sinful pagan Romans, and that, if God is known to exist, certain implications for behavior follow. There is, in short, a scriptural charter for some philosophical inquiries. The believing philosopher, operating within that confidence, does not lose heart as he

---

5. See John Finnis, *Moral Absolutes* (Washington, D.C.: The Catholic University of America Press, 1992).

searches for sound proofs of these matters and confronts the
seemingly overwhelming weight of skepticism in their regard.
The secular philosopher will say that the believer is not willing to
follow the argument wherever it goes, that he cannot in principle
accept as sound an argument that would have it that the human
soul utterly ceases to be at death. Is the secular critic right? Yes.

Christian Philosophy Revisited

Such considerations are reminiscent of what Gilson and Maritain and many others wish to say about Christian philosophy.
Gilson drew attention to the agenda of the believing philosopher,
namely, to provide sound philosophical arguments for truths
whose original habitat is the faith. And he took exception to
those who wished to say, Very well, but once those arguments
are fashioned, we are quite simply in the realm of philosophy and
the fact that truths now known were once believed becomes
irrelevant and accidental. Perhaps we can see more easily now
why Gilson did not wish to accept that consequence. He could
not accept it because he saw philosophy as a life, as a long
complicated process of questioning, reasoning, moving back and
forth over time, encountering difficulties one had not dreamt of
earlier, feeling less confidence than before about some arguments, achieving conviction where none had been before. When
one sees it as a life, as a prolonged dialectical undertaking, the
suggestion that philosophy is a collection of arguments that
somehow just wear their meanings on their faces, will seem bi-
zarre. Let us, Maritain proposes, distinguish between the nature
and the state of philosophy. By the latter, let us mean the activity
of philosophizing considered not episodically but as characteriz-
ing a life, a life that, like any suite of human acts, contains a good
dose of the happenstance and the surprising, a life whose logic is
that sinuous thing Newman tried to describe in the *Apologia* and
spell out in *The Grammar of Assent*. Philosophizing is insepara-
ble from the moral context of the philosopher's life. One who is
pondering the pros and cons of a given argument for the exis-

tence of God is engaged in a type of thinking that can be appraised by appropriate criteria, but his activity is moral as well, a responsible disposition of his time and energy in the context in which he finds himself at the moment. Discourse can be assessed in terms of truth or falsity, but it can also be appraised in terms of one's engagement in it here and now, in these circumstances; in short, a moral appraisal. Nor are these simply parallel appraisals. There are subtle interactions between the moral condition of the thinker and the success or failure of his thinking. Aristotle taught us that, without the moral virtues, the quest for the intellectual virtues will be frustrated.

It is no accident that thinkers who have reminded us of the existential setting of human thought, and thus stressed the pervasiveness of the moral even in the intellectual life, also draw attention to the analogy between ethics and faith. "The reason we have forgotten what it is to be a Christian," Kierkegaard wrote, "is that we have forgotten what it is to be a man." Just as moral character, good or bad, affects our use of our mind and can dispose or indispose us in such a way that the intellectual quest itself fails or succeeds, so believing acceptance of what God in his mercy has revealed to us will affect our engagement in the life of the mind.

What annoyed Gilson, I think, was what he saw as the tendency of believers to apologize for their faith, to wish to reassure their secular fellows that their religious beliefs would not enter into, would not affect and thereby spoil, their philosophizing. It was as if they saw the faith as an embarrassment. At the present time one senses something of this attitude in discussions of Catholic universities. Ignoring the historic character of universities, from their beginnings in the thirteenth century until a relatively short time ago, the question has become: Can our institutions of higher learning be real universities despite the fact that they are Catholic? The very statement of the question appeals to a concept of the university that is to be spurned rather than embraced. Moreover, it reveals a startling ingratitude.

The Christian philosopher is indeed sustained in his activity by his religious faith. Of *course* he will not give credence to arguments that profess to disprove what he believes or what is presupposed by what he believes. No more should any philosopher, confronted with the pyrotechnics of a certain kind of epistemologist, wonder if the room in which the discussion takes place is really there. A philosophical theory that concludes that the world is unreal is existentially and contextually incoherent. To entertain it seriously is to make of philosophy something less than a serious enterprise, to reduce it to the kind of disengaged debating points that too often make up Philosophy 101. There are, then, analogues in the natural order to the believer's unwillingness to be moved by arguments that would undermine the principles on which he lives his life—everyone, including the skeptic, must presuppose the world in which he exists; in addition, the believer accepts truths on the authority of God, and he may be forgiven if he fails to give Bertrand Russell or Richard Rorty pride of place.

This is not, needless to say, obscurantism. Just as any philosopher should be ready to relieve the epistemologist of his imaginary burdens, so the Christian philosopher must be quick to examine arguments that purport to show that the opposite of what he believes is true. His conviction that the argument cannot work does not as such provide him with the correct analysis of its deficiency, and until he has found the latter, he has nothing to offer his secular counterpart that the latter can be expected to accept. But it may be that one of the most fruitful preliminary inquiries in which the Christian and the secular philosopher could engage would concern the question of principles: Are there some things that simply are not up for grabs in philosophy? I have in mind not merely the *tu quoque* the Christian philosopher might level at his secular fellows, but an important shared non-gainsayable truth about the way things are.

Natural Law

Against this background, let us return to what was earlier described as the analogue of the *praeambula fidei* in the practical order, the commandments God gave Moses on Mount Sinai. Thomas holds that the precepts of the Decalogue are ones we could and should know on our own, without any special divine instruction.[6]

> Those precepts pertain to the Decalogue that a man has knowledge of by himself from God. Such are those which can be known straightaway with a little thought from the first common principles, as well as those which are known straightaway by divinely infused faith. Two kinds of precepts are not numbered among those of the Decalogue, namely those which are first and common and need no further promulgation than their being written in natural reason and are self-evident, such as that no man should do harm to another, and the like, and those which the diligent inquiry of the wise discovered to be in accord with reason; . . .

As with *praeambula fidei* generally, these precepts are knowable by natural reason, but unlike those of the speculative order, which are the most difficult to know, coming as they do at the very end and culmination of philosophy, these moral precepts are close to being self-evident, following straightaway from principles that *are* self-evident. This divine sanction for moral precepts, which should be easily grasped, is needed because of the perversity and sinfulness of men whose misbehavior can all but put out the natural light of reason. But that being said, these precepts do not of their nature require the divine sanction, as if they bound us *because* God said so.

One of the reasons the natural moral law is considered to be a

6. "Illa ergo praecepta ad decalogum pertinent, quorum notitiam homo habet per seipsum a Deo. Huiusmodi vero sunt illa quae statim ex principiis communibus primis cognosci possunt modica consideratione: et iterum illa quae statim ex fide divinitus infusa innotescunt. Inter praecepta ergo decalogi non computantur duo genera praeceptorum: illa scilicet quae sunt prima et communia, quorum non oportet aliquam editionem esse nisi quod sunt scripta in ratione naturali quasi per se nota, sicut quod homo nulli debet malefacere, et alia huiusmodi; et iterum illa quae per diligentem inquisitionem sapientum inveniuntur rationi convenire; . . ." (IaIIae, q. 100, a. 3, c).

matter of Catholic doctrine and discipline lies here. The Church is indeed the interpreter and the defender of natural law. Just as the magisterium rightly bears on natural knowledge that is essentially related to the faith, so it must bear on the very principles of moral knowledge. The latter, like the former, is the source of enormous consolation for the believer. Particularly in times when it must seem that no practical agreement is possible between human agents, when theories abound that suggest that moral principles are simply expressions of subjectivity with no objective basis that could ground rational agreement, when it must seem that the most we can hope for is some agreement on morally neutral procedures to adjudicate our moral differences, it is more than merely important to have a certainty that participates in the certainty of faith itself that there is, in their shared nature, a basis for moral agreement among human agents. Whatever the obstacles in the way of that agreement, however complicated and dialectical a process is required for it to come within sight, the believer is sustained by the knowledge that moral agreement can and should be had.

In discussions with secular philosophers, the Catholic philosopher will not of course introduce such considerations as if they were relevant to the desired agreement. The agreement sought will be grounded in what is naturally in the grasp of anyone, however obscured it may have become because of personal and social sin. Just as the relevant verse from Paul will not function as a premise in any philosophical argument for the existence of God, so the fact that a precept is part of the tables of the Law cannot be a philosophical commendation of it.

But surely it will be objected that the cases of the *praeambula fidei* in the usual sense of the term and in the extension of it to truths of the practical order are *not* on the same footing. In the first case, the believer has a sanction external to and prior to philosophy for the claim that the existence of God can be proved from knowledge of the things around us. Fair enough. He must then produce such a proof if he expects to gain the assent of the nonbeliever. He does not, in his philosophical exchange, ask that his interlocutor presuppose the existence of God. In the second case, it is not simply that one claims extraphilosophical sanction for moral precepts naturally knowable. Natural law also requires that the nonbeliever accept the existence of God.

This difficulty does not arise, let us be clear, from the fact that the believer says that he has the sanction of God for precepts that, taken in themselves, require no such divine revelation. The difficulty is rather that what is said to be in the public domain, so to speak, intrinsically depends upon what the interlocutor rejects, namely, the existence of God. How so?

First, there is the very description of natural law when it first comes up in the *Summa theologiae*. It is defined, as we have seen, as the peculiarly human participation in the eternal law. The eternal law is God's providential ordering of his creation. Thus, it would seem that the acceptance of what is called natural law involves the acceptance of the existence of God.

Second, among the precepts of natural law that Thomas enumerates will be found the injunction that we should pursue knowledge of God. It is difficult to see how such a precept could be acted upon without presupposing that there is a God to be known. Thus natural law presupposes that which is not self-evident, which the secular philosopher may be expected to reject and which grounds his suspicion that natural law is, if not disguised Catholic doctrine, certainly a not-so-disguised theism.[7]

A reply to the first difficulty would begin by distinguishing the content of natural law from an account of it, whether philosophical or theological. What the theory of natural law claims is not that each and every human agent can be expected to know the theory or to accept it right off when they hear it explained; rather it claims that there are certain practical judgments any agent can

7. The first objection would be based on *Summa theologiae*, IaIIae, q. 91, a. 2, and the second on q. 94, a. 2: "Tertio modo inest homini inclinatio ad bomun secundum naturam rationis, quae est sibi propria: sicut homo habet naturalem inclinationem ad hoc quod veritatem cognoscat de Deo, et ad hoc quod in societate vivat. Et secundum hoc, ad legem naturalem pertinent ea quae ad huiusmodi inclinationem spectant: utpote quod homo ignorantiam vitet, quod alios non offendat cum quibus debet conversari, et cetera huiusmodi quae ad hoc spectant."

be expected to make. That these judgments are discusssed by the philosopher on an analogy with the first principles of reasoning is true, but such a discussion is arcane. So too, the theological description of natural law as the human agent's peculiar participation in eternal law is not what every agent is taken to know. That is a sophisticated account, the acceptability of which depends on many things. But the burden of the sophisticated account is that every person, sophisticated or not, bears within him the wherewithal to distinguish good from evil.

This answer to the first objection seems to sharpen the difficulty contained in the second. If the theory of natural law sees precepts based on inclinations of our reason and speaks of a natural inclination to know God, it looks as if every human agent from the outset is taken to have knowledge of God. In response it can be said that, in a sense, that is indeed so.

The short shrift Thomas gives the Anselmian argument, an argument that takes the existence of God to be self-evident, so much so that the attempt to deny it must be incoherent, does not prepare one for his lengthy discussion of the suggestion that God is the first thing grasped by our mind.[8] Given the fact that Thomas's favorite scriptural text when he speaks of natural law is Psalm 4.6: "The light of thy countenance is sealed upon us, O Lord" (with natural law being the light of natural reason which enables us to distinguish good and evil), his rejection of the claim that we first know God based on the divine influx of light in our mind is of interest. "But this won't work, because the first light that divinely flows into the mind is the natural light through which the intellective power is constituted. But this light is not what is first known by the mind or the knowledge whereby its quiddity is known, since much inquiry is needed to know what the intellect is; nor is it the knowledge whereby that it is, is known, since we perceive that we have an intellect only in so far

8. The quick dismissal of the ontological argument can be found in *Summa theologiae,* Ia, q. 2, a. 1, ad 2, and a lengthy discussion of the thesis that God is what we first know, in In *Boethii de trinitate,* q. 1, a. 3.

as we perceive ourselves understanding. . . . No one understands himself to understand except insofar as he understands
some intelligible object."[9]

Nonetheless, we have seen that God is the ultimate end of
human life, that things cannot be willed for the sake of the end
unless the end be known, so that it looks as if knowledge of God
is presupposed by the moral life. But consider this text.[10]

It should be said that although God is the ultimate end attained and the
first in intention of natural appetite, it isn't necessary that he be first in
the knowledge of the human mind that is ordered to the end, but in the
knowledge of the one ordering, as in other things that tend to the end by
natural appetite. He is however known as intended from the beginning
in a certain generality, insofar as the mind desires well being and to live
well, which it will have only when it has God.

God, who is unrestricted, infinite existence, is known implic-
itly whenever any existent thing is known; so too, the desire for
any good thing, any participated goodness, is an implicit desire
for essential goodness. "Thou hast made us for thyself, O God,
and our hearts are restless until they rest in thee." Or, as Chester-
ton put it, the young man knocking on the brothel door is looking for God. So too when Thomas suggests a precept based on
the natural inclination of the mind to know God, he gives this:
Seek knowledge, avoid ignorance.

Thus neither the theological account or description of natural

9. "Sed hoc etiam stare non potest, quia prima lux divinitus influxa in mente
est lux naturalis per quam constituitur vis intellectiva. Haec autem lux non est
primo cognita a mente neque cognitione qua sciatur de ea quid est, cum multa
inquisitione indigeat ad cognoscendum quid est intellectus; neque cognitione qua
cognoscitur an est, quia intellectum nos habere non percipimus, nisi in quantum
percipimus nos intelligere, ut patet per Philosophum in IX Ethicorum. Nullus
autem intelligit se intelligere, nisi in quantum intelligit aliquod intelligibile." *In
Boethii de trinitate,* q. 1, a. 3, c.

10. "Dicendum quod quamvis deus sit ultimus finis in consecutione et primus
in intentione appetitus naturalis, non tamen oportet quod sit primus in cognitione
mentis humanae quae ordinatur in finem, sed in cognitione ordinantis, sicut et in
aliis quae naturali appetitu tendunt in finem suum. Cognoscitur tamen a principio
et intenditur in quadam generalitate, prout mens appetit se bene esse et bene
vivere, quod tunc solum est ei, cum deum habet" (*In Boethii de trinitate,* q. 1, a.
3, ad 4).

law as man's peculiar participation in the eternal law nor the precepts based on inclinations of our proper nature give rise to the objections cited.

Fideism

Perhaps the greatest temptation facing the faith in our times is fideism. Just as what is called Wittgensteinian fideism attracted believing philosophers after decades of having the statement of their beliefs called meaningless, so theologians may be tempted to join in the disparagement of reason and commend the faith as its full alternative. Believers who had been attempting to account for their faith as oddly expressed empirical statements, thus to save their meaningfulness, sighed with relief at the suggestion that religion involved a self-contained language game with its own internal rules and intelligibility with no need to be reduced to some other putatively more basic language game in order to be validated. Wittgenstein was taken to underwrite the view that all that religious language needed in order to be meaningful was to be used by believers. It was as simple as that. And please don't ask that faith be related to any other language, say that of physical objects.

That avenue is closed to the Catholic. It is part of our belief that the faith is intelligible, that however obscure and veiled to us now, the object of faith is not only consistent with what we can know, but far exceeds it in intelligibility. The object of faith is *Prima Veritas*. Faith is not an invitation for reason to go on holiday, to leap into the absurd, to engage in Tertullian-like excess. The *preambula fidei,* on both the speculative and the practical level, are part of the package, and they commit us to the truth that there is a necessary connection between faith and reason.

Kierkegaard, in those pseudonymous works meant to trace the path "Away from philosophy!" correctly saw that the mysteries of faith cannot be deduced from what can be known. Any such claim would be rationalism.[11] But Kierkegaard's pseudonym did not see that the relationship between faith and reason is asymmetrical.[12] Faith may not be deducible from reason, but the faith implies and presupposes reason. Merely historical facts about Christ's earthly existence may not entail that he was divine as well as human, but belief in Christ entails historical beliefs. That is why the defense of reason is not merely an option for the Church and for the theologian.

In one of his theological tractates, Boethius advised his reader: *fidem rationemque coniunge.*[13] Yet, when he had been condemned to death by Theodoric, the Ostrogoth king of Italy, unjustly accused of treason, and his fellow senators showed the cowardice we associate with that office, Boethius wrote *The Consolation of Philosophy* while awaiting execution. It is a marvelous book, alternating prose and poetry, and it asks, in effect, the question: Why do the ways of the wicked prosper while the innocent suffer? Boswell tells us that Dr. Johnson expressed wonder we must all feel that Boethius, in such circumstances, showed himself to be *magis philosophus quam Christianus* (more philosopher than Christian). What the concept of Christian philosophy properly understood enables us to see is that one can be *magis philosophus quia Christianus* (more a philosopher because a Christian).

11. In listing three ways in which we can be mistaken about the relation between faith and reason, Thomas includes this: "Secundo ex hoc quod in his quae sunt fidei ratio pracedit fidem, non fides rationem, dum scilicet aliquis hoc solum vult credere quod ratione potest invenire, cum debeat esse e converso; unde Hilarius: 'Credendo incipe, scilicet inquire, percurre, persiste'" (*In Boethii de trinitate,* q. 2, a. 1, c).

12. I am thinking of *Philosophical Fragments* and *Concluding Unscientific Postscript to the Philosophical Fragments,* both attributed to Johannes Climacus (the hero of the unfinished story mentioned above). See *The Point of View of My Work as an Author* for the movements "Away from the poet!" and "Away from philosophy!"

13. The remark occurs at the end of the theological tractate bearing the extensive title, *Utrum Pater et Filius et Spiritus Sanctus de Divinitate Substantialiter Praedicentur?* Boethius is addressing the Deacon John to whom the opusculum is dedicated. "Haec si se recte et ex fide habent, ut me instruas peto; aut si aliqua re forte diversus es, diligentius intuere quae dicta sunt et fidem si poterit rationemque coniunge." *Boethius, The Theological Tractates,* ed. H. F. Stewart, E. K. Rand, and S. J. Tester (Cambridge: Harvard University Press, 1973), p. 36, ll. 68–71.

Bibliography

Aristotle. *L'Ethique à Nicomaque*. Intro., trans., and comm. by R.A. Gauthier and J.Y. Jolif. 2d ed. Louvain: Publications Universitaires; Paris: Béatrice-Nauwelaerts, 1970.

Bazán, Bernardo Carlos. *Siger de Brabant. Quaestiones in tertium de anima. De anima intellectiva. De aeternitate mundi*. Louvain: Nauwelaerts, 1972.

Chenu, M.-D. *Introduction à l'étude de Saint Thomas d'Aquin*. Paris: Vrin, 1954.

Collins, James. "Toward a Philosophically Ordered Thomism." *The New Scholasticism* 32 (1958): 301–26.

Finnis, John. *Moral Absolutes*. Washington, D.C.: The Catholic University of America Press, 1992.

Gilson, Etienne. *The Spirit of Mediaeval Philosophy*. Trans. A.H.C. Downes. New York: Charles Scribner's Sons, 1936.

————. *History of Christian Philosophy in the Middle Ages*. New York: Random House, 1955.

La Philosophie Chrétienne. Journées d'études de la Société Thomiste, Juvisy, 11 Septembre 1933. Juvisy: Les Editions du Cerf, 1934.

Maritain, Jacques. *Science and Wisdom*. Trans. Bernard Wall. New York: Charles Scribner's Sons, 1940.

McInerny, Ralph. *Thomism in an Age of Renewal*. New York: Doubleday, 1966, and Notre Dame: University of Notre Dame Press, 1968.

————. *On There Being Only One Intellect*. Translated, with an introduction and commentary, Lafayette, Purdue University Press, 1992.

————. *Aquinas on Human Action: A Theory of Practice*. Washington, D.C.: The Catholic University of America Press, 1992.

Nelson, Ralph. *Jacques Maritain's Conception of Moral Philosophy Adequately Considered*. Doctoral dissertation, University of Notre Dame, 1961.

Richard, Lucien, O.M.I. *Is There a Christian Ethics?* New York: Paulist Press, 1988.

Smith, Janet E. *Humanae Vitae: A Generation Later*. Washington, D.C.: The Catholic University of America Press, 1992.

Van Steenberghen, Fernand. *La philosophie au XIIIe siècle*. Louvain: Nauwelaerts, 1966.

————. *Aristotle in the West: The Origins of Latin Aristotelianism*, trans. Leonard Johnston. 2d ed. Louvain: Nauwelaerts, 1970.

Wagner, David L., ed. *The Seven Liberal Arts in the Middle Ages*. Bloomington: Indiana University Press, 1986.

Wippel, John, "Thomas Aquinas and the Problem of Christian Philoso-
phy." *Metaphysical Themes in St. Thomas Aquinas,* pp. 1–31. Wash-
ington, D.C. : The Catholic University of America Press, 1984.
————. "Etienne Gilson and Christian Philosophy." in *Twentieth-
Century Thinkers,* ed. John K. Ryan, pp. 59–87. Staten Island: Alba
House, 1965.
Wulf, Maurice De. *Histoire de la philosophie médiévale,* 6th ed. Lou-
vain: Nauwelaerts, 1936.

Index

The Question of Christian Ethics was composed in Sabon
by Yankee Typesetters, Inc., Concord, New Hampshire, and
designed and produced by Kachergis Book Design,
Pittsboro, North Carolina